STUDENT UNIT GUIDE

NEW EDITION

AQA A2 Accounting Unit 3

Further Aspects of Financial Accounting

Ian Harrison

Philip Allan, an imprint of Hodder Education, an Hachette UK company, Market Place, Deddington, Oxfordshire OX15 0SE

Orders
Bookpoint Ltd, 130 Milton Park, Abingdon, Oxfordshire OX14 4SB
tel: 01235 827827
fax: 01235 400401
e-mail: education@bookpoint.co.uk
Lines are open 9.00 a.m.–5.00 p.m., Monday to Saturday, with a 24-hour message answering service. You can also order through the Philip Allan website: www.philipallan.co.uk

ISBN 978-1-4441-7206-5

First printed 2013
Impression number 5 4 3 2 1
Year 2017 2016 2015 2014 2013

Cover photo: Fotolia

Typeset by Integra Software Services Pvt. Ltd., Pondicherry, India

Printed in Dubai

Hachette UK's policy is to use papers that are natural, renewable and recyclable products and made from wood grown in sustainable forests. The logging and manufacturing processes are expected to conform to the environmental regulations of the country of origin.

P3139

Contents

Content Guidance

Questions & Answers

Getting the most from this book

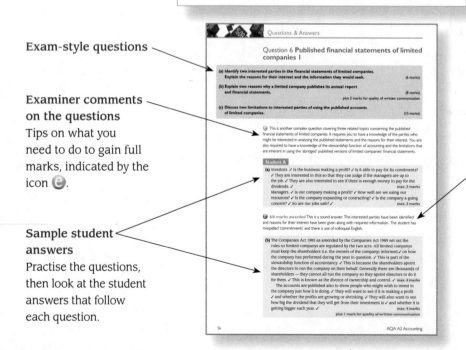

Examiner tips
Advice from the examiner on key points in the text to help you learn and recall unit content, avoid pitfalls, and polish your exam technique in order to boost your grade.

Knowledge check
Rapid-fire questions throughout the Content Guidance section to check your understanding.

Knowledge check answers
1 Turn to the back of the book for the Knowledge check answers.

Summary

Summaries
● Each core topic is rounded off by a bullet-list summary for quick-check reference of what you need to know.

Questions & Answers

Exam-style questions

Examiner comments on the questions
Tips on what you need to do to gain full marks, indicated by the icon ⓔ.

Sample student answers
Practise the questions, then look at the student answers that follow each question.

Examiner commentary on sample student answers
Find out how many marks each answer would be awarded in the exam and then read the examiner comments (preceded by the icon ⓔ) following each student answer.

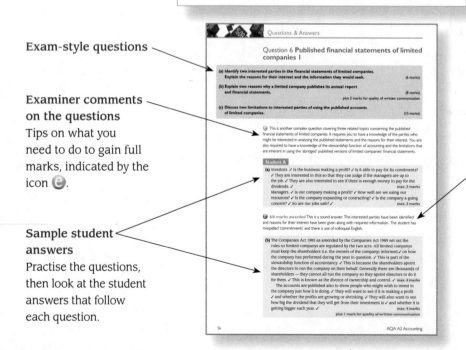

About this book

This student guide is an ideal resource for your revision of AQA Accounting A2 Unit 3: Further Aspects of Financial Accounting.

The guide is in two sections:
- **Content Guidance** covers the content of Unit 3.
- **Questions and Answers** provides ten questions; each question focuses on a specific area of content. Each question is based on the format of the A2 examination papers and is followed by two sample answers (an A-grade and a lower-grade response) together with comments by the examiner.

You should read the relevant topic area in the Content Guidance section before you attempt the question from the Questions and Answers section. Only read the specimen answers after you have attempted the question yourself.

Aims of the A2 qualification

The A2 accounting course aims to encourage you to develop:
- an understanding of the importance of effective accounting information systems and an awareness of their limitations
- a critical approach to the appraisal of financial issues and business practices
- an understanding of the purposes, principles, concepts and techniques of accounting
- the transferable skills of numeracy, communication, ICT, application, presentation, interpretation, analysis and evaluation in an accounting context
- an appreciation of the effects of economic, legal, ethical, social, environmental and technological influences on accounting decisions
- a capacity for methodical and critical thought, which serves as an end in itself, as well as a basis for further study of accounting and other subjects

Content Guidance

The Content Guidance section of this guide outlines the topic areas covered in Unit 3.

Unit 3 builds on the assessment objectives covered in your AS course but the assessment objectives will now be applied to more complex situations and content. (See 'Synoptic assessment' on p. 35.)

On completion of the unit you should be able to:

- assess the available types of business finance
- calculate the profit or loss for a business using the 'net asset method'
- prepare financial statements based on incomplete records
- prepare financial statements for partnerships, including detailed income statements showing how profits or losses are appropriated
- prepare capital and current accounts for partners
- account for structural changes in partnerships
- account for partnership dissolutions
- identify and show an understanding of the main elements of published annual reports of limited companies and be aware of any limitations of these reports
- prepare schedules of non-current assets
- prepare a statement of cash flows
- show an appreciation of the International Accounting Standards (IAS) listed on page 11 of the specification. Don't worry, a detailed knowledge is not required (with the exception of IAS 7 Statement of cash flows); you do need to understand how these affect the information presented in a set of financial statements
- use the FIFO and AVCO methods of determining inventory values
- reconcile inventory values with actual goods held as inventory

Sources of finance

Finance is generally needed to start up a business. The owners may require further finance some time later in order to expand, to replace non-current assets or even to ensure survival if the business is unable to meet some of its commitments.

An unincorporated business (i.e. sole trader or partnership) may use the proprietors' **personal savings** when finance is required. Clearly, in most cases, this type of finance is limited. Few people have an unlimited reservoir of private funds.

Many entrepreneurs seek the help of **family or friends** to help finance a new business. Often, these providers of finance may require some form of security for their investment. This may lead to the provider of finance being given a partnership. However, when a provider of finance is linked to a partnership, this means that all the partners will have unlimited liability, putting at risk not only their investment but also private assets.

Overdrafts are a means of short-term finance. An overdraft is a temporary facility provided by all clearing banks. It allows the business to withdraw funds in excess of the current balance. The bank must agree an overdraft limit before the balance at the bank becomes a debit. Interest is calculated on the overnight overdraft. Interest is charged on an authorised (agreed) overdraft at a lower rate than if the overdraft has not been previously agreed (unauthorised). The rate of interest charged tends to be higher than that charged on loans; for this reason, overdraft finance is generally only used for short-term borrowing. The overdraft provider may cancel an overdraft facility at any time without notice.

Bank loans are available to businesses that can satisfy the lender that the funds will be used for investment purposes and that the business's cash flow will enable capital and interest payments to be made on time. Banks generally require some form of collateral, so loans are often secured on the assets of the business (or, in the case of sole traders or partnerships, on private assets). Interest is charged on the full amount of the loan, whether it is used or not.

A **mortgage** is a long-term loan generally used to purchase property. The provider of the finance uses the property being purchased as collateral to secure the loan. If a business fails to make the required payments, the lender has the right to sell the property to recoup their money.

Trade and other payables provide short-term finance for many businesses. However, excessive use of this type of finance can lead to problems. Individual creditors may insist on cash purchases or may refuse to supply goods if the credit period taken is excessive.

Shares are issued by limited companies to raise finance. Permanent share capital — both ordinary share capital and preferred share capital — together with the company's reserves is known as the equity of the company.

Ordinary shareholders are paid dividends if there are profits available after debenture interest and dividends on preferred shares have been paid. If the company is wound up, the ordinary shareholders are entitled to the funds that remain after the payables, debenture holders and preferred shareholders have been repaid.

Preferred shareholders are entitled to receive a fixed rate of dividend each year, but only if the company has earned sufficient profit. Most preferred shares are cumulative preferred shares, meaning that if dividends have not been paid in earlier years, the arrears will be paid when sufficient profits are available. Preferred dividends are payable before ordinary share dividends and, in the case of a winding up, preferred share capital will be repaid before that of the ordinary shareholders.

Debentures are long-term loans to a company. The loan is generally secured on the assets of the company. Debenture holders are entitled to a fixed amount of interest per annum. Interest is payable whether or not the company has made a profit. If the company fails to pay the interest when it is due, the debenture holders are entitled to have the secured assets sold to pay the outstanding interest and to repay the loan. At the end of an agreed period, the capital sum will be repaid to the lender.

Probably the most important source of finance for any business is the retention of **profits** within the business. This source will ensure that the business is self-financing. If a business has to rely on regular injections of external finance, the implication is that it is not profitable and this will result ultimately in its liquidation.

Knowledge check 1
Explain the difference between a bank loan and an overdraft.

Trade payables is the collective term for trade creditors, who are suppliers who are owed money for purchases of goods for resale. **Other payables** is the generic term for other monies owed.

Examiner tip
All types of shares that are not redeemable are part of equity. Redeemable preferred shares will appear in a statement of financial position as non-current liabilities.

Knowledge check 2
Explain the difference between ordinary shares and preferred shares.

Knowledge check 3
Equity capital comprises all shares, debentures and reserves. True or false?

Examiner tip
Never say that debentures are shares. They are loans to a company. Do not say that reserves are cash. They are profits held back in the company.

Summary

- Finance is important when starting a business.
- Finance is also necessary for the continued survival of the business.
- There are many ways that a business can raise finance.
- Some methods are available only to limited companies: for example, finance raised by issuing shares and debentures.
- Other forms of finance are available to all types of business.
- Sources of finance can be short term or long term.

- Short-term sources include overdrafts and the use of trade credit provided by payables.
- Many sources of finance are external to the business, but businesses can also be funded internally by using retained profits.
- Share capital is provided by shareholders (the owners of a company) who receive dividends when profits and cash are sufficient.
- Holders of debentures (loan capital) are not owners and receive interest whether or not the company is profitable.

Incomplete records

There are two main types of question that are based on businesses that do not maintain a full set of accounting records. It is important that you are able to quickly recognise each of the types. The clue to recognition is seen in the 'required' part of the examination question.

Questions that require you to *calculate* the organisation's profit or loss will use what is called the 'net asset value' method. You should be able to complete this type of problem fairly quickly. Despite what many students think, this is a very accurate method of determining the profit or loss that the business has made. Students sometimes think that in order to determine the profit or loss made by a business, an income statement must be prepared. This is not the case.

Although the net asset method will give an accurate profit or loss for the period under review, it lacks the detail that may be necessary to fulfil the two reasons for preparing financial statements:

- the management function — the net asset method provides no details to help managers determine whether performance could be improved by, say, changing the location of the business premises, changing petrol-driven delivery vehicles to vehicles powered by diesel etc.
- the stewardship function — there are no details to help, say, a bank to determine whether the finance it has provided is being used wisely and safely

The net asset method

There are five stages in the process:

Stage 1 Calculate the value of the net assets of the business. This is also the value of the proprietor's capital. Total the value of all the business assets then deduct the total of all the business liabilities. This will give you the net asset value of the business (i.e. the worth or capital invested in the business).

Stage 2 Using the same method as in stage 1, calculate the value of the net assets (worth or capital) at the end of the period.

Examiner tip

Look at the 'required' part of a question first; this will determine what your answer should contain. Remember the trigger words for incomplete record questions:

- 'calculate' = use of 'net asset' method
- 'prepare' = use of detailed 'T' accounts to give all the necessary details.

Examiner tip

Write items on your script as you key them into your calculator. If you make an error but have not written the results down, you cannot be rewarded for the parts that are correct. Show all your workings. In the 'heat' of the examination, many candidates make simple errors.

Stage 3 Deduct the opening capital from the closing capital. This will give the amount of profit (or loss) retained in the business over the period.

Stage 4 Add the drawings to the retained profits. Drawings are profits that the proprietor has withdrawn from the business for their own personal use.

Stage 5 Deduct any injections of capital into the business. These will have increased the worth of the business; however, this increase in worth is not the result of business activity and so must be disregarded in our calculation of business profits.

We can summarise the five stages thus:

	Closing capital
Deduct	Opening capital
Gives profit retained within the business	£# # # # # # # #
Add	Profits taken from business (drawings)
	£# # # # # # #
Less	Capital introduced into the business
Profit for the year	£# # # # # # #

Remember, this type of question will ask you to *calculate* the profit or loss. It will not ask you to prepare an income statement.

Example:

Aysha's capital at 1 November 2011 amounted to £43 782; at 31 October 2012 her capital was £47 671. During the year ended 31 October 2012 she withdrew £16 500 cash from the business for her own private use; she also purchased a car costing £9400 for her own private use using the business bank account. In April 2012 a relative died, leaving Aysha a legacy of £8500, which she paid into the business bank account.

Calculate the profit or loss earned by Aysha's business for the year ended 31 October 2012.

Answer:

		£
	Closing capital	47 671
Less	Opening capital	43 782
	'Retained' profit	3 889
Add	Profits withdrawn during year	25 900
		29 789
Less	Capital introduced during the year	8 500
	Profit for the year ended 31 October 2012	21 289

Preparation of detailed financial statements

The second type of problem is *the preparation of detailed financial statements from fragmentary records*. This happens when the proprietor of a business does not keep a full set of accounting records. Often, in reality, only a cash/bank book is maintained in detail.

Knowledge check 4

What is another name for net assets?

Content Guidance

The key to solving this type of problem is found again in the 'required' part of the examination question. These questions will always require you to *prepare* an income statement.

Once again there are five stages. It is important that you learn the five stages and that you always follow them in a logical, careful way:

Stage 1 Prepare an opening statement of financial position on the first day of the year using information given in the question. (This is, in fact, an opening **statement of affairs**, since if a set of ledgers is not maintained there can be no information from which to prepare a statement of financial position.) You should be able to do this almost as quickly as you can write. Do not categorise the items, just total the assets and then deduct the liabilities. Do this quickly and neatly. Only draw up a formal statement of financial position using the relevant headings if this is required in the question.

Stage 2 Prepare a bank transactions summary (this is generally given in the question).

Stage 3 Prepare a summary of cash transactions.

Stage 4 Construct adjustment (or total) accounts (many teachers call these control accounts).

Stage 5 Using the information calculated in stages 1–4, select the necessary information and prepare an income statement and a closing statement of financial position using this information.

Always follow the five stages methodically and carefully, showing them in as much detail as you can. These are your workings — and if you make an error in determining a figure that appears in your answer, you will most probably earn part marks for the correct parts of your workings.

The part of the process that seems to give most people a few problems is stage 4. The figures taken straight from the summaries of cash and bank transactions do not take into account the accruals concept. The concept tells us that, as accountants, we record the value of the use of resources to the business, not the cash paid to acquire the resources.

You will generally need to prepare adjustment accounts to determine the sales and purchases for the year under consideration. You will generally also have to prepare further adjustment accounts for some of the business expenses.

There are two methods of making the adjustments used to determine the figures to be used in the income statement. Either is acceptable — use the method you feel most comfortable using.

Example:

The following information is given for Hetal:
Cash received from credit customers	£7650
Cash paid to credit suppliers	£34 670
Cash paid to landlord for rent	£3060

	at 31 December 2012	at 1 January 2012
	£	£
Trade receivables	210	180
Trade payables	8790	6780
Rent owed	120	60

Examiner tip
Learn the five stages — they are so important.

A **statement of affairs** is another term for a statement of financial position when using the 'net asset' method of calculating the profit or loss of a business.

Knowledge check 5
Identify two sources of additional capital that might be introduced into a small business.

Knowledge check 6
Which of the following transactions should be classified as drawings? Money paid: for family holiday; for purchase of new television set for home; to son for work done in business; for insuring delivery vehicle.

AQA A2 Accounting

Calculate the sales and purchases for the year ended 31 December 2012 and the rent to be included in the income statement.

Answer:

Trade receivables total account

							£
Bal b/d	180	Cash	7650		Cash		7650
Inc stat	7680	Bal c/d	210	alternative method	Closing balance		210
	7860		7860				7860
Bal b/d	210				Opening balance		(180)
					Sales		7680

Trade payables total account

							£
Cash	34670	Bal b/d	6780		Cash		34670
Bal c/d	8790	Inc stat	36680	alternative method	Closing balance		8790
	43460		43460				43460
		Bal b/d	8790		Opening balance		(6780)
					Purchases		36680

Rent account

							£
Cash	3060	Bal b/d	60		Cash		3060
Bal c/d	120	Inc stat	3120	alternative method	Closing balance		120
	3180		3180				3180
		Bal b/d	120		Opening balance		(60)
					Rent		3120

These adjustment accounts are necessary because of the accruals concept, so do them carefully and in detail. Do not take short cuts. If you do, you are more likely to make errors and errors cost marks. Some students are initially unsure how many adjustment accounts to open and use. If you are unsure, open an adjustment account for every item shown on your opening statement of financial position and any extra items listed in your bank and cash summaries. This might appear to be going over the top but you must not leave anything to chance during the examination. The inventories are adjusted in the trading section at the start of your income statement when you calculate your cost of sales.

As you gain more confidence with practice, you will probably notice that some of the non-current asset accounts do not change or only change because of the depreciation charge, so you may not wish to open an adjustment account in these cases.

Where appropriate, put the 'balancing' figures from your adjustment accounts into the income statement. Any balances brought down in your adjustment accounts are shown in the statement of financial position.

Stage 5 involves using all the relevant figures that you have calculated in the previous four stages.

Examiner tip

If you use adjustment accounts to find the figures for your income statement, put the closing balances under the account and 'bring them up' into the account.

Knowledge check 7

Wages paid during the year £77 360. Wages owed at beginning of year £1340. Wages owed at end of year £1450. What is the entry in an income statement for the year for wages?

Summary

- The profit for the year can be calculated by comparing the net assets held by a business at the end of a financial year with the net assets held at the start of the year.
- This is a very accurate way of determining profit (provided that the values placed on assets and liabilities are accurate).
- The major drawback with using this method is that it does not provide the detail that may be necessary for the stewardship and management functions of accounting.

- If a 'full set' of financial statements is required then the five-step approach must be applied:
  - Prepare an opening statement of affairs.
  - Prepare a summary of all bank transactions (generally given in the question scenario).
  - Prepare a summary of all cash transactions.
  - Construct detailed adjustment (total) accounts (many teachers call these control accounts).
  - Using the information calculated in the previous four stages, prepare an income statement and statement of financial position.

Financial statements of partnerships

The financial statements of all businesses are similar in most respects. A manufacturing business will produce an additional manufacturing statement (examined in Unit 4) then an income statement.

Because the profit for the year has been earned by more than one person, the income statement must be extended to show how the profit has been shared between the partners.

It is usual for a partnership to draw up a partnership agreement. This can avoid disputes in the future with regards to the partners' duties and responsibilities and their share of profits or losses made by the business.

If there is no partnership agreement then the Partnership Act 1890 lays down some basic rules that apply:

- Partners are to contribute equal amounts of capital.
- No partner is to be entitled to interest on capital or be charged interest on drawings.
- No partner is to be entitled to a salary.
- Residual profits are to be shared equally.
- Any loans to the business by partners will carry interest at 5% per annum.

In an examination question, if no details are given as to how profits are to be shared, you must assume that the Partnership Act comes into play and profits should be shared equally with no other **appropriations** of profits.

A partnership statement of financial position also differs slightly from that of a sole trader. Since there is more than one owner in a partnership, there must be more than one capital account showing the financial involvement of each of the partners. In many cases, the capital employed in a partnership business is further divided into capital accounts and current accounts.

Examiner tip

If there are no details of how profits are to be shared, you must assume that no partnership agreement exists, so the Partnership Act 1890 applies to the question.

The **appropriation** section of an income statement shows the users of financial statements what has happened to the profits of the business.

Capital accounts detail:
- deliberate injections of capital — generally, this means the capital introduced when a partner initially enters the business plus any further injections as and when the business might require further funds
- goodwill adjustments
- any profits or losses that arise through the revaluation of assets

The last two components will arise only when there is a structural change in the composition of the partnership.

Current accounts detail:
- all entries relating to the current year's profit or loss (including withdrawals of profits by the partners — drawings)
- any adjustments necessary to correct errors in the distribution of the previous year's profits or losses

As the owners of a business, partners receive profits. Although we may label the profits as salaries, interest on capital and residual profit, remember that they are all part of the overall profit for the year. If a question asks how much profit a partner has earned, you will need to add the three parts together.

Example:

Tom is in partnership with Mildred. The following is an extract from the partnership income statement.

		£	£
Salary	— Tom		7000
Interest on capital	— Tom	3000	
	— Mildred	6000	9000
Share of residual profit			
	— Tom	18152	
	— Mildred	27228	45380
Total profit for the year			61380

Calculate the profit earned by Tom during the year.

Answer:

Tom earned £28152 (£7000 + £3000 + £18152)

Structural changes

Structural changes occur when:
- a new partner is admitted
- a partner leaves the partnership or retires
- there is a change to the profit(loss)-sharing ratios of the partners
- the partnership is dissolved (see below)

The key to success is to remember that you must prepare two sets of financial statements to record the changes brought about:
- a set that records all the transactions occurring up to the date of the change
- a set that records any transaction that occurs after the date of the change

---

Knowledge check 8

'Current accounts' is another name for the capital accounts shown on a partnership statement of financial position. True/false?

Knowledge check 9

Explain why partners might wish to maintain both capital accounts and current accounts.

When a structural change takes place, the assets of the business need to be valued. The assets of the business shown on the statement of financial position at that date may not be a true reflection of their worth. (Remember that assets are valued at cost on a statement of financial position because of the going concern concept.)

The assets can be revalued since at the date of the structural change, the business ceases to be a going concern. The profit/loss on revaluation belongs to the original partners in the pre-change residual profit-sharing ratios.

Goodwill is the amount by which the value placed on a business exceeds the value of the business's assets and liabilities.

When a successful partnership is restructured, generally the partners will agree a value to be placed on the goodwill of the business. Goodwill is an intangible non-current asset that should appear in the statement of financial position of the 'new' business. However, in examination questions, you will generally be asked to write off goodwill.

Example:

Aysha and Bert are in partnership, sharing profits and losses in the ratio 2:1 respectively. Their financial year end is 31 December.

Chung is admitted to the partnership at the close of business on 30 April 2012. He contributed £20 000 as his capital and share of goodwill. The new profit-sharing ratios are 3:2:1.

The summarised partnership statement of financial position at 30 April 2012 showed:

		£
Net assets		45 000
Capital accounts — Aysha	25 000
— Bert	20 000
		45 000

The partners agree the following asset values:

Net assets	£48 000
Goodwill	£39 000

Prepare a statement of financial position at 30 April 2012 after the admission of Chung as a partner.

Answer:

Aysha, Bert and Chung summarised statement of financial position at 30 April 2012

		£
Net assets		68 000
Goodwill		39 000
		107 000
Capital accounts	A	53 000
	B	34 000
	C	20 000
		107 000

If the goodwill account is not to be maintained in the books of account of the 'new' partnership, it should be written out of their books of account. The above statement of financial position would appear thus:

		£	
Net assets		68000	
Capital accounts	A	33500	(53000 – 19500)
	B	21000	(34000 – 13000)
	C	13500	(20000 – 6500)
		68000	

When a partner leaves the partnership, a similar process of revaluation is followed at the date of the change. Any goodwill to be written off would then be debited to the remaining partners in the 'new' business.

Remember that you are dealing with two businesses: the 'old' partnership 'sells' all of its assets to the 'new' partnership. The assets will be 'sold' at what the business might fetch if the business was being sold on the open market (i.e. at the value of the assets plus a value placed on the goodwill of the business).

Partnership dissolution

When a partnership is dissolved the assets of the business are disposed of and any liabilities are settled. The liabilities are settled in the following order:
1 payables
2 partners' loans
3 partners' capital accounts

You should transfer any current accounts into the respective partners' capital accounts.

Do not transfer partners' loans into the respective partners' capital accounts. Settle these, immediately after you have paid the amounts due to payables, using the business bank account.

You need to be able to prepare a realisation account for the partnership.

On the debit side	On the credit side
Carrying amount of the assets	What the assets are sold for
Discounts allowed	Discounts received
Costs of dissolution	
Profit on realisation	Loss on realisation

The profit (or loss) on realisation should be posted to the partners' capital accounts.

The *Garner* v *Murray* rule applies if a partner is unable to settle his or her debt to a partnership after dissolution. Any deficiency is shared between the other partners in the ratio of the balances in their capital accounts shown in the last statement of financial position.

Any balances remaining on the partners' capital accounts should then be transferred to the bank account remaining in the books of account. After these transfers have been made, both the capital accounts and the bank account should balance.

Examiner tip
The most common error in preparing a realisation account is to put items on the wrong side of the account. The carrying amount for the assets appears on the debit side; what they fetch is entered on the credit side.

Transfer price is the value at which shares in a private limited company (Ltd) are exchanged.

A, B and C share profits in the ratio 3:2:1 respectively. On the last statement of financial position capital account, balances were £10000; £20000; and £30000. After all entries have been made on the dissolution of the partnership, there remains a debit balance of £3000 on the capital account of A. A is unable to settle this balance. How should this balance be dealt with?

Do not try to divide the bank balance up in the profit-sharing ratios — this is a common error made by students. If you have completed your debits and credits accurately, the bank account and the capital accounts should disappear after this set of transfers. Try to make all the entries carefully and methodically and the whole question should balance out.

Sometimes some assets are taken over by a limited company. You will be told what the purchase consideration is and how it is made up. The tricky part is the calculation regarding the value of the shares to be distributed between the partners.

Example:

Frurto Ltd takes over some of a partnership's assets. The purchase consideration is £500000 made up as follows:

£100000 cash
£150000 debentures
50000 ordinary shares of £1 each in Frurto Ltd

Prepare the account of Frurto Ltd as it would appear in the partnership books of account.

Answer:

Frurto Ltd

		£			£
Assets		500000	Cash		100000
			Debentures		150000
			Ordinary shares		250000
		500000			500000

Purchase consideration £200000 comprising £10000 cash, £40000 debentures and 60000 ordinary shares of £1 each. What is the transfer price of each ordinary share?

The cash is debited to the bank account.

The debentures are debited to the partners in the ratio given in the question.

The £250000 for ordinary shares is debited to the partners' capital accounts in the ratios given in the question.

So what has the 50000 got to do with the question, you may ask? This is the number of shares issued to the partners. These shares have a value of £250000 to the partners, so each share must have a market value of £5.

Summary

- A partnership exists when two or more people are in business together.
- A partnership should have a partnership agreement. If no agreement exists, the Partnership Act 1890 lays down the rules that govern the partnership.
- The income statement of a partnership will contain an appropriation section that details how profits (and losses) are shared.
- Partnerships can maintain fixed or fluctuating capital accounts.
- Most partnerships maintain fixed capital accounts. All appropriations of profits are entered in current accounts, together with withdrawals of profits (drawings).
- Entries in capital accounts involve capital transactions only.

- When a structural change takes place in a partnership business, two appropriation accounts should be prepared; one showing the transactions that took place before the change, the second showing the transactions that took place after the change.

- When a structural change takes place, the business should be valued and, if appropriate, a value should be placed on goodwill.

- When goodwill is introduced, the value is shared between the 'old' partners in the 'old' profit-sharing ratios.

- If goodwill is not to remain in the business books of account, it is written out of the books of account and the 'new' partners are debited with a share of its value in the 'new' profit-sharing ratios.

- When a partnership is wound up, assets are debited to a realisation account. The account is credited with the amounts for which the assets are sold. The profit (or loss) is calculated and transferred to the partners in their profit (loss) sharing ratios.

- Any loans from the partners to the business should be paid off using the partnership bank account.

- Current accounts should be closed by transferring their balances to the respective partners' capital accounts.

- Capital accounts are closed by a transfer of cash.

- If a partner is insolvent, any debit balance on their account is shared between the remaining partners in the ratio that reflects the balances shown on the last statement of financial position.

Published financial statements of limited companies

You will not be required to prepare an income statement or statement of financial position for a limited company in a format suitable for publication. Nor will you be required to prepare notes to the accounts other than a schedule of non-current assets.

The financial statements that you could be asked to prepare for limited companies follow, in the main, the financial statements that you have been preparing for sole traders and partnerships. These financial statements would be used for internal purposes only as part of the management function of accounting. An 'abridged' version is available for anyone to inspect and to fulfil the management function of accounting.

The corporate report (annual report and financial statements) is made available to every shareholder. It contains:
- an income statement
- a statement of financial position
- a statement of cash flows
- a statement of changes in equity
- notes to the financial statements
- a statement of the company's accounting policies
- the directors' report
- the auditors' report

Knowledge check 12

Explain why a public limited company (plc) prepares an 'abridged' version of its financial statements for publication.

The directors' report

The directors of a limited company have a responsibility to ensure that the provisions of the Companies Act 1985 are implemented and that the financial statements are prepared in accordance with the Companies Act and that appropriate accounting standards are applied.

The responsibility is to ensure that the company's records:
- show and explain the company's transactions
- show the financial position of the company
- give a true and fair view of the financial position of the company
- contain daily records of cash transactions
- record the assets and liabilities of the company
- detail inventories held at the year end

The directors must ensure that the statutory accounts are produced and filed with the Registrar of Companies.

A director must sign the annual financial statements on behalf of the board, once they are approved by the board.

The auditors' report

Knowledge check 13

'The auditors of a limited company are responsible for the everyday running of the company. They are appointed by the directors, who are the owners.' Comment on this statement.

Larger companies must have their financial statements audited by external auditors. The auditors are appointed by the shareholders. The published statements contain the auditors' report. The report has three sections:
- Respective responsibilities of directors and auditors — the directors' responsibilities are to prepare the annual report, the directors' remuneration report and the financial statements. The auditors' responsibility, on the other hand, is to audit the financial statements and remuneration report and to form an opinion.
- Basis of audit opinion — this section outlines the framework of standards under which the audit was conducted and a summary of the methods used when conducting the audit.
- Opinion — this gives the auditors' opinion as to whether the financial statements present a true and fair view of the company's activities. If the auditors are of the opinion that certain aspects of the financial statements have not been dealt with correctly, they will give a qualified opinion.

The published statements should be prepared in accordance with IAS 1 Presentation of financial statements. This standard sets out how financial statements should be presented, which enables comparisons to be made with previous accounting periods and with other companies.

IAS 1 lays down the minimum detail that must be shown in the financial statements:
- income statement
- statement of financial position
- statement of changes in equity
- statement of cash flows
- accounting policies

However, in answers to examination questions, you will probably have to show more detail than that shown in a set of published financial statements. Your answers will resemble summarised financial statements prepared for internal use.

You should be aware of the many user groups who have an interest in the published financial statements of limited companies and what their interest would focus upon. Most users of accounts are interested in the survival of the business and this depends on the ability of the business to generate profits and to have a consistent cash flow.

The user groups would include:
- teachers and students
- bank managers — will wish to know that any investment that their bank has made is secure and that repayment(s) will be made when due
- HM Revenue and Customs — will be interested in the results of the business to ensure that the correct amount of tax is paid
- employees — will be interested in job security (a successful business will ensure this)
- customers — will be interested in the continued supply and delivery of goods
- suppliers — will wish the business to succeed so that repayment of outstanding or future debts can be made. They also hope that they will continue to receive orders

You should also be aware that the information given in a set of published financial statements is limited in nature. You should be able to discuss these limitations. For example:
- The statements are prepared using historic cost and are therefore already out of date.
- The statements give an overall view of the company — some parts of the business may be more/less efficient than others but this is not apparent from a scrutiny of the published statements.
- Comparisons with other businesses may be difficult since different organisations have different structures and policies, which may not be evident from the published statements.
- They may be biased — they are prepared by the directors — and tend to show only monetary aspects of the business. They cannot, for example, show whether or not the workforce is motivated or content.

Schedule of non-current assets

You should be able to produce a schedule of non-current assets. This will show in detail the movements in non-current assets over the financial year and the detail of accumulated depreciation and impairment losses.

Example:

The directors of CDE plc provide the following information regarding freehold property for the year ended 30 November 2012.

Freehold property at cost   £302 000
Aggregate depreciation   £56 000

During the year:
- the company purchased property at a cost of £3000
- the company sold freehold property that cost £5000 and had a carrying amount of £1000

It is company policy to charge depreciation on freehold property at 2% per annum on cost.

Impairment occurs where the carrying amount (cost less aggregate depreciation) of a non-current asset is greater than its recoverable amount.

Prepare a schedule of non-current assets for freehold property for the year ended 30 November 2012.

Answer:

Freehold property

Cost or valuation	£
At start of period	302 000
Additions	3 000
Disposals	(5 000)
At end of period	300 000

Accumulated depreciation and impairment losses

	£
At start of period	56 000
Charge for period	6 000
Disposals	(4 000)
At end of period	58 000
Carrying amount:	
At end of period	242 000

For comparative purposes, the previous year's schedule is given prior to the current year's schedule in a company's annual report.

Knowledge check 14

At beginning of the financial year: vehicles at cost £140000. During the year a new vehicle was purchased for £20000. An old vehicle with a carrying amount of £12000 was traded in for £6000 and £14000 cash was paid. Prepare a schedule of non-current assets for vehicles.

Statements of cash flows

You will not be required to have a detailed knowledge of any of the International Accounting Standards *apart from IAS 7*. This is the standard dealing with how a business has raised cash and how it has used its cash over a financial year.

Income statements concentrate on how profits (or losses) have arisen over the financial year. The long-term survival of a business depends on its profitability.

As the name implies, a statement of financial position shows the financial position of the business at a particular moment in time by listing the assets and how the business is financed.

Examiner tip

Learn the content of the IASs listed in the specification plus the number and the name (see pp. 26–31).

A statement of cash flows shows:
- cash inflows and cash outflows, since cash inflows are essential for short-term survival
- information that is not disclosed in the other two financial statements
- information that enables the users of financial statements to assess how well cash and cash equivalents have been used during the year
- information that enables an assessment of liquidity, viability and financial adaptability of the business to be made

It also allows comparisons to be made year-on-year or inter-firm, because IAS 7 requires a prescribed format so that such comparisons can easily be made.

In examinations, questions requiring a statement of cash flows are always based on two statements of financial position for a business (generally a limited company). Remember that the managers of any business might find it in their best interest to prepare a statement of cash flows. Since cash is essential to the short-term survival of all businesses, even though a statement of cash flows is not a statutory requirement for small companies and unincorporated businesses, the preparation of a statement of cash flows would indicate how money has been acquired and spent.

Limited companies are required by IAS 7 to produce a statement of cash flows as part of their end-of-year financial statements. IAS 7 requires the following format headings:
- operating activities
- investing activities
- financing activities

Statements of cash flows are prepared by comparing the amounts shown in the latest statement of financial position with the amounts shown in the statement of financial position prepared one year earlier.

You may have to undertake some calculations to determine the cash flows involved in the acquisition and disposal of non-current assets.

Learn the subheadings above and remember to use a full heading (no abbreviations at all). There are often two presentation marks attached to this type of question.

Do not forget that, in your statement of cash flows, outflow amounts are always shown in brackets. For example:

	£000	£000
Cash flows from investing activities		
Purchases of non-current assets	(1 270)	
Proceeds from sale of non-current assets	120	
Cash (used in)/from investing activities		(1 150)

This shows a cash outflow of £1 270 000 for the purchases of non-current assets while a cash inflow of £120 000 was received from the sale of non-current assets. The overall result from investing activities was a net cash outflow of £1 150 000.

Operating activities

Remember that cash and profits are not the same thing. A business may be profitable yet have less cash at the end of the year than it had at the start of the year. Conversely a business can make a loss yet have more cash at the year end than it had a year earlier.

Test yourself on how this could happen.

Cash flows from operating activities are the main revenue-producing activities of the company. They are the cash inflows and cash outflows that result from the 'normal' trading activities of the business. To determine this figure we use figures from the income statement and from a comparison of consecutive years' statements of financial position.

> **Knowledge check 15**
>
> A statement of cash flows forecasts whether or not the business will require overdraft facilities in future months. True/false?

> **Examiner tip**
>
> The operating and investing activities show the 'internal' generation of cash flows. The financing activities show the extent of the 'external' generation of finance.

The total of cash flows from operating activities comprises the following:

Profit from operations (profit for the year before interest and tax)

Plus total depreciation for the year
Plus loss on sale of non-current assets   *or*   *Deduct* profit on sale of non-current assets
Plus decreases in inventory   *or*   *Deduct* increases in inventory
Plus decreases in trade receivables   *or*   *Deduct* increases in trade receivables
Plus increases in trade payables   *or*   *Deduct* decreases in trade payables

If positive, this total gives cash from operations. If negative, the total shows cash used in operations.

There are two further adjustments. Both are deducted from the cash flows resulting from operations:
- deduct interest paid during the year
- deduct tax paid during the year

Investing activities

Cash flows shown under this heading are those resulting from:
- the disposal of non-current assets — these cash inflows are the receipts from sales of all types of non-current assets (including investments)
- the purchase of non-current assets — these cash outflows are the payments made to purchase all types of non-current assets (including investments)
- interest received from investments
- dividends received from investments in other companies

Financing activities

Under this heading we find all receipts from and payments to all external providers of finance.

Cash inflows will result from:
- share issues (both ordinary shares and preferred shares)
- issues of debentures
- taking out long-term loans

Do remember that overdrafts will be part of the cash and cash equivalents, so will not feature under this heading.

Cash outflows will be the result of:
- payments to redeem both ordinary shares and preferred shares
- payments to redeem debentures that have reached term
- repayments on long-term loans
- dividends paid to both ordinary shareholders and preferred shareholders

The three subtotals of:
- cash (used in)/from operating activities
- cash (used in)/from investing activities
- cash (used in)/from financing activities

are totalled to give:
- the net increase/(decrease) in cash and cash equivalents

(You can quickly check if this total is correct. It should equal the difference in the cash and cash equivalents at the start of the year and the cash and cash equivalents at the end of the year.)

Finally, the cash and cash equivalents from the statement of financial position at the beginning of the year is added to the net increase/(decrease) in cash and cash equivalents to give the figure for cash and cash equivalents shown in the statement of financial position at the end of the year.

The reconciliation of the movement in cash to the movement in net debt shows all the cash flows that affect the net debt position. It reconciles the net debt at the beginning of the year with the net debt at the end of the year.

Example:

Net increase in cash and cash equivalents over the year £327 500:

	31 December 2012	1 January 2012
	£	£
7% debenture stock	600 000	700 000
Long-term bank loan	150 000	150 000
Cash and cash equivalents	233 500	6 000

Prepare a statement reconciling net cash flow to movement in net debt.

Answer:

Reconciliation of net cash flow to movement in net debt

	£
Increase in cash in the period	327 500
Net debt at 1 January 2012 (700 000 + 150 000 – 6 000)	(844 000)
Net debt at 31 December 2012 (600 000 + 150 000 – 233 500)	(516 500)

There are a number of calculations required to calculate cash flows that may cause difficulties.
- Depreciation is added to the profit from operations because depreciation is a non-cash expense that reduces profit but does not result in cash leaving the business.
- Similarly, the profit generated by the disposal of a non-current asset is a book entry and should be deducted from the profit from operations. The cash received resulting from the sale will be shown as a cash inflow under investing activities. (Note: a loss on disposal has the opposite effect — that is, it should be added to the profit from operations.)
- Calculation of the annual provision for depreciation charged to the income statement means that the aggregate amount of depreciation will have increased by this amount over the year. If the aggregate depreciation at the beginning of the year is deducted from the aggregate amount at the end of the year, the answer should be the annual charge. However, examiners often complicate things. You may have to construct 'T' accounts to find the annual charge. (See the example below on disposals of non-current assets.)
- Calculation of cash flows is required when there is a disposal of a non-current asset. When a non-current asset is sold, you may have to calculate the cash flows that result.

Cash and cash equivalents are cash in hand plus bank balances plus short-term investments that are convertible into cash without notice.

Net debt is the borrowings of a limited company less its cash and liquid resources. (Liquid resources are current asset investments held as readily disposable stores of value, i.e. short-term deposits.)

Knowledge check 18

Depreciation is shown as a cash inflow in a statement of cash flows because it is the cash put aside in order to replace a non-current asset in the future. Comment on this statement.

Example:

The following are extracts from the statements of financial position of SMH plc:

	at 31 May 2012	at 31 May 2011
	£000	£000
Non-current assets at cost	746	787
Less depreciation	172	195
	574	592

During the year ended 31 May 2012, non-current assets that had cost £120000 were sold for £9000. The non-current assets sold had been depreciated by £108000.

Identify any entries in a statement of cash flows that result from the information given.

Answer:

Use 'T' accounts to give a fuller picture of all the transactions.

By inserting the given information into the 'T' account it is obvious that the account does not balance.

Non-current assets account

	£		£
Balance b/d	787000	Disposal	120000
Missing figure		Balance c/d	746000
	866000		866000
Balance b/d	746000		

The missing figure must be due to the purchase of further non-current assets. So, cash outflow £79000 is to be entered under the heading of investment activities.

Depreciation of non-current assets account

	£		£
Disposal	108000	Balance b/d	195000
Balance c/d	172000	*Missing figure*	
	280000		280000
		Balance b/d	172000

So £85000 depreciation (the 'missing figure') has reduced the current year's profit but has not depleted cash. £85000 must be added to the profit from operations under the heading operating activities.

Disposal of non-current assets account

	£		£
Non-current assets	120000	Depreciation of non-current asset	108000
		Bank	9000
		Loss on disposal	3000
	120000		120000

This gives two entries to be made in the statement of cash flows: a cash inflow of 'actual' cash £9000 and a 'book entry' cash inflow of £3000. This loss has reduced the profit from operations but has not taken cash from the company. £3000 has to be added to the profit from operations under the heading 'operating activities'.

**An extract from the statement of cash flows for
SMH plc for the year ended 31 May 2012**

	£000
Operating activities:	
Operating profit:	
Depreciation charges for the year	85
Loss on disposal of non-current assets	3
Investing activities:	
Purchases of non-current assets	(79)

The following two items will alter a company's statement of financial position but will have no impact whatsoever on the statement of cash flows.
- Treatment of a revaluation of non-current assets. A revaluation of non-current assets is not reflected in a statement of cash flows since there is no movement of cash. The revaluation is merely a book entry that:
  – increases the value of non-current assets
  – increases the value of reserves in the company's statement of financial position
- Treatment of a bonus issue of shares will alter the company's statement of financial position. There will be an increase in the ordinary share capital but there will be an equivalent reduction in the company's reserves; no cash changes hands. There is no entry in the statement of cash flows.

Summary

- The financial statements that are produced for use of directors and managers of a limited company are similar in many respects to the financial statements produced by sole traders and partnerships.
- The published financial statements should be prepared in accordance with IAS 1 Presentation of financial statements. This standard sets out how financial statements are to be presented.
- The directors' report summarises the principal activities of the company.
- Directors must ensure that the provisions of the Companies Act 1985 are adhered to; that the company's records are maintained in detail and that they show a 'true and fair view' of the company's financial affairs.
- Auditors are appointed by the shareholders and they must form an opinion as to whether or not the published financial statements do show a 'true and fair view' of the company's activities.
- You may be asked in the examination to discuss the topics covered in the directors' and auditors' reports.
- A schedule of non-current assets shows the changes that have taken place during a financial year. It details the changes in each type of non-current asset held; the changes in the accumulated depreciation charges and impairment losses. It summarises for each type of asset the carrying amount at the date of the statement of financial position.
- IAS 1 requires limited companies to publish a statement of cash flows as part of their financial statements.
- IAS 7 requires a standard format using the headings:
  – Operating activities
  – Investing activities
  – Financing activities
- All cash movements are shown in the statement.
- Transactions that do not involve a movement of cash or cash equivalents (e.g. issues of bonus shares and revaluation of non-current assets) are not part of a statement of cash flows.

International Accounting Standards

'Why is there a need for International Accounting Standards?' you may ask. The answer is that they provide the ground rules on which businesses will prepare and present any accounting information.

The setting of standards:

- ensures consistency of presentation
- enables comparability with the company's financial statements of previous years
- enables comparisons with the financial statements of other companies
- is useful for management purposes but does have some limitations
- can be useful for potential investors
- is useful for current investors who can readily see how the company is shaping up
- helps to prevent directors from covering up any poor results etc.

Increasingly, the financial world is shrinking and many investors are now investing in overseas businesses. When making decisions on whether to invest in a UK company or one overseas, it is essential that like is compared with like. The implementation of International Accounting Standards helps to achieve this.

There are ten International Accounting Standards covered in the AQA specification. You do not have to have a detailed knowledge of nine of these standards. The one exception is IAS 7 Statements of cash flows.

You must learn the number of each standard and its title, for example 'IAS 2 Inventories'. You do not have to memorise the whole standard by heart, but you must know how the standard will affect the composition and preparation of financial statements.

Knowledge check 19

Explain why International Accounting Standards should be applied in the preparation of financial statements.

IAS 1 Presentation of financial statements

This standard sets out how financial statements should be presented. It requires that financial statements must state clearly that they comply with international standards. This means that comparisons can be made with the company's financial statements from previous periods and with the financial statements of other companies.

IAS 1 lists the complete set of financial statements as:

- a balance sheet (statement of financial position)
- an income statement (statement of comprehensive income)
- statements of changes in equity
- a statement of cash flows
- a statement summarising accounting policies and other explanatory notes

The standard aims to ensure that the financial statements provide and present useful information about the company's financial position and performance as well as its cash flows. It lays down the minimum disclosure requirements and stipulates that comparative information is shown.

Financial statements

IAS 1 requires that financial statements are prepared annually and that they adhere to some of the basic concepts that you are already familiar with, i.e. going concern; accruals basis of accounting; consistency of presentation; materiality and aggregation and offsetting. If you have forgotten these basic concepts, you should revisit them in your textbook or class notes to familiarise yourself with them again.

1 The statement of financial position

IAS 1 requires that non-current assets are clearly shown separately from current assets and that non-current liabilities are separated from current liabilities. It also requires the details of the components of the equity of the company.

You will not be required to prepare a set of financial statements for publication. As a result, much of the detail given in an examination question will have to be included in your answers.

2 The income statement (statement of comprehensive income)

The standard lays down the minimum requirements of items to be shown. These include revenue, finance costs, tax expense and the profit or loss (note that the word 'net' has disappeared).

Once again, examination questions are likely to have more detailed entries than those shown in a set of published financial statements.

3 Statement of changes in equity

The statement must show:
- the profit or loss
- changes to any of the components of equity

4 Notes to the financial statements

- Information must be given about the basis of preparation of the financial statements.
- Information must be included regarding specific accounting policies used in the preparation of the financial statements.
- Information must be given about the amount of proposed dividends and the related amount per share.

Other items that must be shown in the income statement or in the statement of changes in equity or in the notes include:
- the amount of dividends paid during the year
- the amount of dividend paid per share

> **Examiner tip**
>
> You must learn the content of the IASs listed in the specification plus the number and name (see pp. 26–31). You may have to apply the appropriate standard to the detail in a question.

> **Equity** is the term used to describe permanent share capital (ordinary and preferred shares) plus all reserves.

IAS 2 Inventories

This standard is frequently tested. Inventories are assets that are held for sale in the ordinary course of business. Inventories should be valued at the lower of cost and net realisable value.

Cost includes taxes, import duties, transportation costs, any costs of conversion and any other costs incurred in bringing the goods to their present location and condition.

Net realisable value is the estimated selling price less any costs incurred in the making the goods available for sale.

IAS 2 accepts inventories valued using:
• First in first out (FIFO) basis
• Weighted average cost (AVCO) basis

IAS 7 Statement of cash flows

See pages 20–25.

IAS 8 Accounting policies, changes in accounting estimates and errors

IAS 8 gives more detail than IAS 1 with regard to accounting policies. When a policy is given in a specific standard it must be applied in the preparation of financial statements; they must be applied with consistency in similar situations. If a change in policy is required, this must be noted in the financial statements.

IAS 8 also deals with errors and changes in estimates if a material error is discovered or a material change to the carrying amount of an asset or liability is required. It should be corrected in the next set of financial statements by adjusting the comparative figures.

IAS 10 Events after the reporting period

These are events that occur after the statement of financial position has been prepared but before the financial statements are authorised for issue.

Adjusting events require changes to the financial statements before they are authorised whereas non-adjusting events do not. For example, if a credit customer that owed a significant debt goes into liquidation shortly after the year end, the financial statements should be adjusted to reflect this. Proposed dividends at the year end are a non-adjusting event, since they require shareholders' approval at the AGM.

IAS 16 Property, plant and equipment

IAS 16 covers recognition, the carrying amount of the asset and depreciation charges.

Plant, property and equipment should be recognised as assets when future economic benefits are received and the cost of the asset can be measured reliably. The asset should initially be recorded at cost (cost is the purchase price plus all costs needed to get the asset into working condition).

The standard allows the assets to be valued at cost after acquisition less accumulated depreciation and impairment losses, or at revaluation based on its fair value at the revaluation date less subsequent depreciation and impairment losses. When a revaluation results in an increase in value, a revaluation reserve should be entered in the statement of financial position as part of equity.

Fair value is the amount for which an asset could be sold less costs incurred to secure a sale.

Depreciation

The purpose of providing depreciation is to reflect the cost of using an asset. Annual depreciation should be charged to the income statement. Depreciation is not affected by repairs and/or maintenance; these are revenue expenses. However, they may affect the lifespan and/or the residual value of the asset.

The residual value and the useful life of an asset should be reviewed each year and if there are material changes from previous estimates, IAS 8 requires that the changes should be recorded in the financial statements.

Derecognition occurs when an asset is disposed of or is obsolete. Any gain or loss on disposal should be entered in the income statement.

For each class of asset, the financial statements must show the following (generally, the detail is shown in the notes to the financial statements):
- the basis for determining the carrying amount
- the depreciation method used
- the useful economic life or rates of charging depreciation
- the carrying amount
- the accumulated depreciation and impairment losses at the beginning and end of the accounting period
- a reconciliation of the carrying amount at the beginning and end of the accounting period that shows:
  - additions
  - disposals
  - revaluations
  - impairment losses
  - depreciation

Depreciation is the apportioning of the cost of a non-current asset over its useful economic life.

Examiner tip
Do not say that depreciation is the fall in the value of an asset.

Knowledge check 20
Identify an accounting concept that is applied to the provision for depreciating a non-current asset.

IAS 18 Revenue

IAS 18 defines revenue as the gross inflow of economic benefits that arise from the normal operating activities of the business. So, revenue is income from:
- sales of goods (or services)

- royalties
- interest or dividend income

Revenue is recognised when the seller has transferred to the buyer the risks and rewards of ownership.

The accounting policy for recognising revenue is detailed in the notes to the financial statements. The amount of each of the following types of revenue should be shown in the notes:
- sale of goods
- rendering of services
- interest
- royalties
- dividends

IAS 36 Impairment of assets

You need to understand the following terms.

Impairment occurs when a non-current asset's carrying amount is greater than its recoverable amount.

Carrying amount is the value of a non-current asset shown in a statement of financial position after the deduction of accumulated depreciation and accumulated impairment losses.

Recoverable amount is the higher of a non-current asset's fair value and its value in use.

Fair value is the amount for which a non-current asset could be sold less any costs incurred in the sale.

Value in use is calculated by discounting the future cash flows generated by the use of a non-current asset.

Impairment occurs when the value of a non-current asset shown on the statement of financial position is greater than the larger of the discounted cash flows generated by the non-current asset or its value if sold.

Impairment losses should be shown in the income statement.

Knowledge check 21

Carrying amount of non-current asset £140000; fair value £100000; discounted value in use £120000.

Calculate the impairment loss.

IAS 37 Provision, contingent liabilities and contingent assets

You need to understand the following terms:

Provision is an amount set aside out of profits for a known expense, the amount of which is uncertain.

A liability is an existing obligation to make a payment that has resulted from a past event.

A contingent **liability** is a possible obligation that may occur if a future uncertain event takes place.

A **contingent asset** is a possible asset that might arise from past events.

Contingent indicates that something may take place.

IAS 38 Intangible assets

An intangible asset does not have physical substance.

Intangible assets are shown in the financial statements at cost. Intangible assets with a finite life are amortised over their useful lives. Intangible assets with an indefinite life are not amortised but they should be tested annually for impairment.

Internally generated goodwill and internally generated brand names are not recognised as assets.

Research and development costs are treated as revenue expenditure when incurred. However, if development costs can be shown to be part of an intangible asset that can be sold or used by the company to generate future incomes, then these costs can be capitalised.

Knowledge check 22

Identify two intangible assets.

Summary

- International standards are the ground rules by which accounting records are produced.
- Application of accounting standards ensures that all financial statements are prepared with consistency.
- This allows comparisons with other businesses to be made more easily.
- It facilitates year-on-year comparisons within the same business.
- With the exception of IAS 7 Statements of cash flows, you do not need to memorise the wording of the standards.

- You should know the number and title for each standard and the broad outlines of what is covered.
- You need to know how each standard affects the preparation of financial statements, and you could be asked to identify the application (or non-application) of a standard to a particular scenario given in a question.
- The general principles must be thoroughly understood so that they can be applied to a variety of business problems.

Inventory valuation

Remember, the overriding principle to be used at all times is that inventory should be valued at the lower of cost and net realisable value.

The only two methods of valuing inventory that are examined (and that are acceptable for IAS 2) are:
- First in first out (FIFO)
- Weighted average cost (AVCO)

You could be asked to calculate the closing inventory for a business using either of these two methods.

Some businesses keep detailed records of inventory transactions, making entries every time goods are received and issued. This method of recalculating inventory value after every transaction is known as **perpetual** inventory valuation.

Knowledge check 23

Which of the following are acceptable methods of valuing inventories: AVCO; FIFO; LIFO; LILO?

Explain the difference between a perpetual method of valuing inventory and a periodic valuation. Give an example of a business that would use each method.

A business has a uniform mark-up of 50% on all goods sold. The business owner was unable to value his inventory on his year end 30 April. The inventory was valued at £54000 on 7 May. Between 1 and 7 May, goods costing £800 were purchased and sales valued at £900 were made. Calculate the value of inventory held at 30 April.

Other businesses only value their inventory at the end of a financial period (generally their year end); this is known as **periodic** inventory valuation.

Always use the periodic method when using FIFO as it is much quicker and it requires minimum calculation. You must use the perpetual method when calculating closing inventory using AVCO. The methods that you use will give differing inventory valuations, and so each method will give a different gross profit figure. As a rule the higher the inventory value, the higher the gross profit (the lower the valuation, the lower the gross profit).

You may be asked to calculate the value of inventory at a financial year end when the value of inventory is physically checked some days after the year end. If a physical inventory check was conducted on 7 November after the financial year end on 31 October, any goods sold between 1 and 7 November would still have been held by the business at 31 October. The cost price of these goods needs to be added to the inventory value at 7 November. Conversely, goods purchased in the week up to 7 November should not be included.

Some questions may ask you to calculate the gross and/or profit for the year after you have calculated the inventory. Remember, if you increase the value of closing inventory, you will increase reported gross profit (and also profit for the year) by the amount of the increase. If you decrease the value of closing inventory, you will decrease reported gross profit (and profit for the year) by the amount of the decrease.

Summary

- FIFO and AVCO are methods of valuing inventory. They are regularly examined at A2.
- They are methods of valuation, and do not necessarily determine the order in which goods are dispatched to customers or other departments.
- The FIFO method can be calculated using either a periodic method or a perpetual method.
- If a question does not require you to use a perpetual method when using FIFO, then use a periodic calculation. It is quicker and easier and so you are less likely to make a computational error.
- There is no right or wrong way to value inventories but some are acceptable under accounting standards.
- The method of valuation chosen will determine the level of reported profit.
- When inventories are valued some time after the end of the financial year, a statement showing the necessary adjustments must be prepared.

Questions & Answers

In this section of the guide there are ten questions. Each question is followed by two sample answers interspersed with comments from the examiner.

The questions are typical of those you could be faced with in your A2 examination. Some of the questions will test your ability to solve a numerical problem using knowledge, understanding and application skills. Other questions will involve some analysis and then an evaluation of the scenario.

Sample answers

In each case, the first answer (by student A) is intended to show the type of response that would gain a grade A. Remember that a grade-A response does not mean that the answer is perfect. You will see that there is a range of marks that could score a grade A.

The answers given by student B illustrate the types of error that weaker students tend to make, thus depriving them of vital marks that could easily have moved their script up into another grade boundary.

In the sample answers, each point awarded a mark is shown with a tick ✓. Where you see ✓*, this indicates that the mark has been awarded for the student's own figure, i.e. although the final figure is incorrect, it is based on the correct method.

Resist the temptation to look at these answers before you attempt the question.

Examiner comments

Examiner comments on the questions are preceded by the icon ⓔ. They offer tips on what you need to do to gain full marks.

Examiner comments on the sample answers are preceded by the icon ⓔ. In some cases they are shown within the student's answer, but in the main they appear after the student's answer. In weaker answers, the comments point out areas for improvement and the type of common error found in answers that are around the pass/fail boundary.

Assessment

Remember that the course is designed to allow you to show your ability and to use your skills. All the accounting examination papers test the following assessment objectives in the context of the specification content to varying degrees:

- **knowledge and understanding** of the accounting principles, concepts and techniques within familiar and unfamiliar situations
- **application** of knowledge and understanding — of all the accounting content that is covered in the course — to familiar and unfamiliar situations
- **analysis and evaluation** by ordering, interpreting and analysing information using appropriate formats, taking into account the possible effect of all factors, internal and external, to the business — making judgements, decisions and recommendations

based on the assessment of alternative courses of action that might be influenced by internal and external factors

Quality of written communication (QWC)

On each paper, 4 marks are awarded for the quality of written communication. The marks are split equally between written communication (for prose answers) and quality of presentation (for numerical answers). These marks are awarded in specific questions that are clearly identified on the examination paper.

The specification requires that you use:
- text that is legible, and that your spelling, punctuation and grammar ensure that the meaning is clear
- a form and style of writing that is appropriate to the purpose and to the complexity of the subject matter
- information in a clear, coherent way and that specialist vocabulary is used where appropriate

Unit 3

Unit 3 contributes 25% of the marks for the A-level qualification. It is a 2-hour written paper and there are 90 raw marks available. There will be four compulsory questions. Each question will have a variable number of sub-questions and will carry a variable number of marks.

The approximate weightings for Unit 3 are:

Knowledge and understanding	20%	17 marks
Application	50%	43 marks
Analysis and evaluation	30%	26 marks
	100%	86 marks (plus 4 marks for QWC)

Compared with AS Unit 1, fewer marks are available for knowledge and understanding and hence more emphasis is required on analysis and evaluation.

You can learn to recognise the marks allocated to the higher-order skills of analysis and evaluation by the use of certain 'trigger' words. The most common trigger words are:
- **Advise** — suggest solutions to a problem and justify your solution.
- **Analyse** — identify the characteristics of the information given.
- **Assess** — make an informed judgement based on information supplied in the question.
- **Discuss** — present advantages and disadvantages or strengths and weaknesses of a particular course of action and arrive at a conclusion based on the question scenario.
- **To what extent** — similar to 'discuss' but requiring a judgement based on the likelihood of potential outcomes and effects on the given scenario.

It is important that answers requiring analysis and evaluation result in a judgement being made. You use these skills almost every day. For example, you might say to a friend, 'I think we should go bowling tonight because...' — that is a judgement. You might add to that an analysis of the reasons why you think you should go bowling: '...because the lads we met there last time said that they would be there tonight too and we had such a good time with them last week'.

Synoptic assessment

Synoptic assessment tests your ability to see relationships between different topic areas included in the subject content. It will be tested by using decision-making or problem-solving situations where you will be required to draw together knowledge and understanding of content areas learned in different parts of your A-level accounting course. In Unit 3 you will be tested on issues relating to Units 1 and 2.

Stretch and challenge

There is a requirement at A2 that you should be stretched to reach your full potential and be presented with questions that present a challenging situation. This will be achieved in questions that require evaluation and the application of knowledge and skills to complex situations.

Question 1 **Sources of finance**

(a) George is planning to start a business next spring. He has prepared a detailed business plan that shows that he requires £80 000 start-up capital.

REQUIRED

Discuss two methods that George should consider to raise the required capital. (12 marks)

(b) Neal-Harrison plc is an established company that has been trading for several decades. Additional finance amounting to £2.5 million is required to expand its present operations.

REQUIRED

Discuss two methods of raising the necessary finance that the managers of Neal-Harrison plc should consider. (12 marks)

plus 2 marks for quality of written communication

ⓔ In this common type of written question it is always useful to prepare a plan of the points to be considered. The plan will help you to avoid repeating points; it is also useful to help the flow of your answer — you can arrange your points in the most logical sequence. Remember that the trigger word 'discuss' requires a conclusion at the end of the answer, based on the question scenario. Remember also that sometimes 'obvious' answers will score valuable marks: for example, own savings in this question.

> ### Student A
>
> **(a)** George could use his own savings. ✓ This means that he won't have to find any repayments each month. ✓ Also he will not be charged interest on the money he uses. ✓ However, there is the opportunity cost of the money used ✓ — that is, the interest that he has given up on his savings. ✓ However, this is not going to be much at the moment what with the credit crunch. By using his own cash he will still be the boss of the company, ✓ he will still be in charge ✓ and nobody can tell him what to do or what not to do ✓ — so he can expand if he wants, he can buy and sell what he wants. But this might leave his family short in the future. If his house or car needs repairing he won't have any savings to fall back on. ✓ Also if he needs any more cash to bale out the company where is the money to come from? He has spent £80 000 of savings already. ✓   **max. 5 marks**
>
> George could go into partnership with somebody that has cash to invest. ✓ Once again he wouldn't have to find any repayments ✓ and any interest ✓ and it is fairly permanent — he will have the money until his partner wants to get out of the partnership. ✓ The new partner will perhaps have different skills ✓ and expertise ✓ so this would be good. But he will now not be in soul charge. ✓ It means that if he wants the day off or is ill, there will be someone to cover him. He will have to share profits ✓ if the company makes them (on the other hand, if the company makes losses he will only have to bare half of them). There could be arguments over policy ✓ so he will have to make sure that any partner is a friend or someone he knows.   **max. 5 marks**
>
> I think that his best line would be to go into partnership ✓ as this means that he will be sharing any risks ✓ and it will lighten his workload.   **2 marks**

ⓔ **12/12 marks awarded** This is a comprehensive analysis of the pros and cons of using own savings as a means of financing a business. The student has arrived at a conclusion and has justified it. Attention has been paid to the trigger word 'discuss'. There are some spelling mistakes, and the use of the word 'company' when the student is describing the business of a sole trader is not good. If there had been a mark for quality of communication in this section, the student would have lost a mark. As it is, maximum marks are scored.

(b) The managers of Neal-Harrison plc have a lot more ways of raising finance than George did. This is why people form a limited company. The two best ways of raising extra finance are:

Sell extra shares. ✓ This method will raise the money. They can do it by selling shares to the general public (the company is a plc so they can do this). Because Neal-Harrison is well established this could be fairly straightforward. Because the company is well established it is likely that the shares could be sold at a premium. ✓ So the £1 shares could be sold for say £1.25. ✓ This means that 2 million shares sold would raise the £2.5 million. ✓ This would mean that there would be an extra 2 million votes at the AGM so it would dilute the power of existing shareholders. ✓ If the shares were sold to existing shareholders (this is called a rights issue), ✓ there would not be a loss of any control since the shares are issued pro-rata ✓ (using the same proportions). If the shares were to be used to raise the capital they would have to be paid dividends ✓ (only if they made profits, if they didn't make a profit they would not get any dividend). These ordinary shares will form extra permanent capital and need not be ever paid back ✓ unless the company goes bankrupt and then they will be the last to be paid out.   **max. 5 marks**

The managers could sell debentures. ✓ Debentures are long-term loans to the company. ✓ They have to be paid a set amount of interest each year ✓ so if the debentures are 5% debentures (2025) this means that each debenture holder will get £5 interest for every £100 invested until 2025. ✓ The interest has to be paid even if the company makes losses ✓ so although this is less risky for the investor, it is very risky for the company ✓ if they make a loss. If the company cannot pay the interest then the debenture lenders can seize the assets of the company, ✓ sell them and take back interest money and the amount that they loaned the company. ✓   **max. 5 marks**

I think they should sell more shares ✓ it would raise permanent capital and they don't have to pay anything back in the form of dividends if they don't want to. ✓   **2 marks**

ⓔ **14/14 marks awarded** Student A has developed the answer well when discussing a share issue at a premium and the rights issue. Other good development points were evident when discussing debentures. There were a couple of slips — the use of the word 'bankrupt' and the concept of 'taking back interest' — but otherwise this is a good, well-thought-out answer.

ⓔ **Total: 26/26 marks (grade A)**

Student B

(a) George could use some savings ✓ but he would have to be very rich to do that. This method might mean that he has nothing to fall back on at home. ✓ He would be his own boss ✓ but he would have to close the business if he got swine flu or if he got days off or if he went on holiday. **3 marks**

He could get a bank loan ✓ or overdraft. If he got a bank loan, he would have to pay bits of it all the time until it was paid off. If he did not repay regularly the bank could take his business away and he would have lost everything. With a bank loan the bank manager might interfere with the running of the business ✓ to ensure that there money is safe. **2 marks**

ⓔ **5/12 marks awarded** This answer is too brief. Student B should have realised that it was necessary to write much more to score the maximum 12 marks. There is no attempt to develop the areas covered. The student seems to believe that George would be the only person involved in running the business.

An overdraft would be an inappropriate way to gain finance in these circumstances. The mention of the bank having an interest in the affairs of the business could have been developed. There is no conclusion. The student ought to have known that the trigger word 'discuss' requires a conclusion.

(b) They could sell shares. ✓ This would mean that they got dividends if the company made profits. They would have limited liability. This means that they could only lose the money that they had invested in the first place. If the company does not make a profit they will not get anything. They will have a vote at the AGM so if they don't like the directors they can vote them off. If the share price on the stock exchange rises they can sell there shares at a capital gain (but if it falls they would make a capital loss).

The other type of share is less risky. They are called preferred shares. They always get a dividend and if the company goes bust, then they get their money out first so they are less risky. If they don't get their dividend this year they could get it next year when the company is profitable. **I mark**

I would invest in preferred shares. They are less risky and you always get your money back. **plus I mark for quality of written communication**

ⓔ **2/14 marks awarded** Student B has made a common error of addressing the question from the wrong viewpoint. Whether this was carelessness or whether this is the answer to a question the student hoped might appear, who knows? Only 1 mark can be awarded for content.

ⓔ **Total: 7/26 marks (fail)**

Question 2 **Incomplete records 1**

Archie Barchy is a sole trader. He has not kept a full set of accounting records. However, he is able to provide the following information:

	at 1 January 2012	at 1 January 2011
	£	£
Premises at valuation	80000	80000
Fixtures at valuation	16000	18000
Vehicle at valuation	8000	12000
Inventory	5600	5000
Trade receivables	140	170
Trade payables	2780	3200
Bank balance	760	–
Bank overdraft	–	6400

During the year ended 31 December 2011 Archie's drawings amounted to £18500.

During the year ended 31 December 2012 Archie withdrew £1500 per calendar month for personal use. He also spent £3250 on a family holiday. He took goods valued at £230 for his own private use. In February 2012 Archie's uncle died and Archie paid a legacy of £14500 into the business bank account.

The following additional information is available at 31 December 2012:

(1) An extension to the business premises was built during the year. The extension cost £50000 and was financed completely through a mortgage from the Midvillage Building Society. As yet, no repayment of capital has been paid.

(2) Fixtures have been depreciated by 10%.

(3) The vehicle was replaced in August 2012 with a new vehicle. Archie paid £14000 and received a trade-in allowance of £6000 for the old vehicle. The new vehicle is to be depreciated by 25% per annum on cost.

(4) Trade receivables have been valued at £300 but Archie believes that one customer who owes £90 will be unable to pay his debt.

(5) Trade payables amounted to £3455.

(6) Archie's bank statement shows a debit balance at bank of £2770 at 31 December 2012 but a cheque for £650 had not been presented.

(7) Inventory at 31 December 2012 was valued at £6000. This included damaged goods that cost £500. These goods can be sold for £600 after being repaired at a cost of £350.

REQUIRED

(a) Calculate the profit or loss for the year ended 31 December 2011.   (5 marks)

(b) Prepare a statement of financial position at 31 December 2012.   (24 marks)

plus 2 marks for quality of written communication

(ℯ) This question tests your ability to differentiate between questions that require the preparation of a full set of financial statements and those that require only a calculation to determine the profit or loss made by a business. The question tests your ability to prepare a statement of financial position in good style by categorising assets and liabilities and hence capital.

Student A

(a)

	£
Capital	105 570 ✓
Add profit	20 650 ✓
Less drawings	18 500 ✓
Capital	107 720 ✓ + ✓

(ℯ) **5/5 marks awarded** Student A has used a variation on the net asset method of calculating the business profits, and has used the traditional layout for the capital section of a statement of financial position. This is perfectly acceptable and may indicate that the student feels more comfortable using this approach. The 'extra' mark has been awarded because the subtotal for the profits retained in the business is not shown using this approach. The student should have given a heading. Nevertheless, maximum marks are scored.

(b) **Statement of financial position for A. Barchy at 31 December 2012**

Non-current assets		
Premises	130 000 ✓	
Fixtures	14 400 ✓	
Vehicle	10 500 ✓	14 000 × 0.75 ✓
	154 500	
Current assets		
Inventory	5 750 ✓✓✓	6000 − 600 + 350
Trade receivables	390	
	6 140	
Current liabilities		
Trade payables	3 455 ✓	
Bank overdraft	2 120 ✓	2770 ✓ − 650
	5 575	
Net current assets		565
		155 065
Non-current liabilities		
Mortgage		50 000 ✓
		105 065
Capital		107 720 ✓
Legacy		14 500 ✓
Drawings		(21 480) ✓✓✓
		100 740
Profit		4 325
		105 065

plus 2 marks for quality of written communication (I for a good heading and I for the subheadings 'non-current assets', 'current assets', 'current liabilities' and 'non-current liabilities')

e 20/26 marks awarded This is a good answer with only a few minor errors. The student has been rather careless in calculating the total for non-current assets and the trade receivables figure, and would probably have gained two further marks if workings had been shown. The statement of financial position is well presented and labelled correctly. The capital section is unusually presented but the student's own profit figure was calculated more easily using this approach. However, the addition error in the total of non-current assets meant that the own figure mark could not be awarded.

e Total: 25/31 marks (grade A)

Student B

(a) – (2000) – (4000) + 600 – (30) + 420 + 760 + 6400 = £2150 ✓✓✓

e 4/5 marks awarded This is another unusual approach. The only error is that the student did not adjust the profit figure to take into account the drawings made. Although this is an acceptable approach, the number of calculations involved means that there are far more areas where errors could be made. The answer should always contain a heading to inform the examiner what the student is attempting.

(b)   **Financial position**

Premises		130000 ✓
Fixtures		14000
Vehicles		23000
		167000
CA		
Inventory	6950	6000 ✓ + 600 + 350 ✓ – 230
Trade receivables	300 ✓	
Bank	3420	2770 + 650
	10440	
CL		
Trade payables	3455 ✓	
Depreciation	13200	2000 + 11200
Mortgage	50000	
	66655	
Net current assets		55755
		232755
Capital		2150 ✓*
Add profit		197625
Add legacy		14500 ✓
Drawings		18480 ✓ 15000 + 3250 ✓ + 230 ✓
		232755

ⓔ **10/26 marks awarded** There are many fundamental errors and careless mistakes here. For example, the mortgage and depreciation have been included as current liabilities. There is also a failure to realise that the business had an overdraft. The heading is incomplete and the subheadings are abbreviated or missing. This is a poor effort for an A2 student. The statement of financial position scores 10 marks but the presentation is awarded zero.

ⓔ **Total: 14/31 marks (grade E)**

Question 3 Incomplete records 2

Roger Guillaume did not keep proper accounting records for the year ended 31 December 2012. However, he is able to supply the following information:

Summarised bank account

	£		£
Balance at bank 1 January 2012	1 342	Wages	45 673
Cash banked	139 359	Drawings	17 804
Receipts from credit customers	1 560	Purchases	2 984
		General expenses	13 438
		Purchase of vehicle	21 500
		Payments to credit suppliers	40 078
		Balance at bank 31 December 2012	784
	142 261		142 261

Roger's till rolls reveal that the business takings for the year amounted to £185 754. Before banking the takings, Roger paid wages amounting to £25 461 and rent £7080. He also withdrew £11 720 for his own personal use.

During December the shop was burgled and money was stolen from the till; Roger is uncertain of the precise amount. His insurance company will pay compensation of £2000 on 7 January 2013.

Roger also provided the following information:

	at 31 December 2012	at 1 January 2012
	£	£
Fixtures and fittings at valuation	12 600	14 000
Vehicle at valuation	15 972	5 120
Inventory	16 800	18 400
Trade receivables	156	278
Trade payables	10 132	9 807
Wages owing	1 380	1 230
Rent owing	–	360
Rent paid in advance	480	–
Cash in hand	194	127

REQUIRED

(a) Calculate the amount of cash stolen. (6 marks)

(b) Prepare an income statement for the year ended 31 December 2012. (30 marks)

(c) Prepare a statement of financial position at 31 December 2012. (12 marks)

ⓔ This type of question is very testing because of the detailed calculations (or ledger accounts) that are required to implement the accruals concept. Much information from the workings has to be brought together accurately to prepare the detailed financial statements required.

Student A

(a)

Calculation of stolen cash

Cash in hand at beginning	127 ✓	Payments made	44 261 ✓
Takings	185 754 ✓	Banked	139 359 ✓
		Cash in hand at end	194 ✓
		Missing fig money stolen	2 067 ✓
	185 881		185 881

ⓔ **6/6 marks awarded** This is an excellent, well-laid-out answer that scores maximum marks.

(b)

Workings

Receivables

Bal	278 ✓	Cash	1 560 ✓
I S	1 438	Bal	156 ✓
	1 716		1 716

Payables

Cash	40 078 ✓	Bal	9 807 ✓
Bal	10 132 ✓	I S	40 403
	50 210		50 210

Wages

Cash	45 673 ✓	Bal	1 230 ✓
Bal	1 380 ✓	I S	45 823
	47 053		47 053

Rent

Cash	7 080 ✓	Bal	360 ✓
Bal	480	I S	7 200
	7 560		7 560

Vehicle

Bal	5 120 ✓	Depn	10 648
Cash	21 500 ✓	Bal	15 972 ✓
	26 620		26 620

ⓔ This answer shows good, clear workings. Without these the student would have lost 7 marks, including 4 for wages (the cash paid to employees, £25 461, has been omitted) and the rent paid in advance at the year end has been entered on the wrong side of the account.

R Guillaume. inc statement for the y/e 31 Dec 12

		£	£
Sales	1 438 ✓ + 185 754 ✓		187 192
Inventory		18 400	
Purchases		43 387 ✓✓	
Inventory		16 800 ✓	44 987
			142 205

	£	£
Wages	45 823 ✓	
Rent	7 200 ✓	
General expenses	13 438 ✓	
Depreciation	12 048 ✓✓	
Stolen	2 067	80 576
Profit		61 629 ✓*

ⓔ 25/30 marks awarded This is a good attempt and it is laid out well. However, there are a number of basic errors that have cost the student some simple marks that an A2 student should never throw away.

The income statement heading contains abbreviations. Headings should always be written in full — so 'R Guillaume. Income statement for the year ended 31 December 2012' would have scored the heading mark. There is no label to identify the gross profit. These are two basic errors that a student of this calibre should not be giving away. Students should also label the cost of sales, as examiners sometimes include this as a presentation mark.

The actual 'expense' for the cash stolen is £67 rather than the £2067 that was included.

Note that the asterisk above indicates a mark awarded for the student's own figure.

(c)   **Financial position at 31 Dec 12**

Fixtures		12 600	
Vehicles		15 972	
		28 572 ✓	
Current assets			
Inventory	16 800 ✓		
Receivables	156 ✓		
Bank	784 ✓		
Cash	194 ✓		
Rent in advance	480 ✓		
	18 414		
Payables	10 132 ✓		
Wages owed	1 380 ✓	11 512	6 902
			35 474
Capital		55 679	
Profit		61 629 ✓*	
		5 950	
Drawings		29 524 ✓	
		35 474	

(e) **10/12 marks awarded** This is a neat, well-laid-out statement of financial position. The heading is poor as it again contains abbreviations. There are two computational errors. The payment to be paid by Roger's insurance company should have been included as a current asset. The opening balance on the capital account should have been calculated using the 'net asset' method rather than by using the 'missing figure' technique, which relies on the student preparing a perfect income statement and statement of financial position.

(e) **Total: 41/48 marks (grade A)**

Student B

(a) Cash stolen 185 754 ✓ – 44 261 ✓ = £141 493 ✓*

(e) **3/6 marks awarded** This answer illustrates clearly the importance of showing workings. Without workings, £141 493 would not have scored, but Student B has earned part marks. The answer has not been adjusted to include the opening and closing cash in hand, nor has the cash withdrawn from the till and banked been included.

(b)

	£	£
Sales		185 754 ✓
Inventory	18 400	
Purchases	2 984 ✓	
	21 384	
Inventory	16 800 ✓	4 584
GP		181 170
Less expenses		
Wages	71 134	
Rent	7 080 ✓	
Vehicle	21 500	
General exps	13 438 ✓	
Depn fix	1 400 ✓	
Vehicle	10 648 ✓	
Stolen	141 493 ✓*	245 193
Loss		64 023

(e) **8/30 marks awarded** Here is another example of a student throwing away some easy presentation marks. There is no heading — you must always give a full heading. 'GP' means that the gross profit mark cannot be rewarded. Students should always identify the cost of sales.

The income statement is neat and well presented, although once more the student has used abbreviations. There are two major errors in the income statement that no A2 student should be making at the end of 2 years' study.

First, the student has included the purchase of the vehicle (capital expenditure) in the revenue statement — this is why no 'own figure' mark for the loss has been awarded. In addition, the student has not adjusted the appropriate expenses to take into account the accruals concept as outlined in stage 4.

(c)

Statement of financial position	£	£
Non-current assets		28 572 ✓
Inventory	16 800 ✓	
Receivables	278	
Cash	194 ✓	
Rent	480 ✓	
	17 752	
Payables	(10 132) ✓	
Wages	(1 380) ✓	6 240
Suspense account		1 029
		35 841
Capital		1 342
Loss		64 023
		65 365
Dwgs		29 524 ✓
		35 841

ⓔ **7/12 marks awarded** This is a neat, well-presented statement of financial position. Student B has used the list of assets and liabilities given in the question. This is a useful technique for checking the accuracy of your statement of financial position. However, the heading has no date and the subheadings for current assets and current liabilities are missing.

There are also some basic errors. Because the bank balance was not included in the list, it was omitted from the detail of current assets; the student did include it incorrectly as the opening capital! The loss was added to the student's opening capital when it should have been deducted. The student has used a suspense account to ensure that the statement of financial position balances; avoid this as it serves no useful purpose and simply wastes time that might be more profitably used scoring further marks.

ⓔ **Total: 18/48 (grade E)**

Question 4 Financial statements of partnerships 1

Albert and Bertoli have been in partnership for many years, sharing profits and losses equally. Their statement of financial position at 30 November 2012 is shown:

	£	£
Non-current assets		
Premises	210000	
Machinery	70000	
Vehicles	80000	360000
Current assets		
Inventory	12000	
Trade receivables	20000	
	32000	
Current liabilities		
Trade payables	9000	
Bank overdraft	8000	
	17000	
Net current assets		15000
		375000
Non-current liabilities		
Mortgage on premises		190000
		185000
Capital accounts		
Albert	100000	
Bertoli	80000	180000
Current accounts		
Albert	6000	
Bertoli	(1000)	5000
		185000

At the close of business on 30 November 2012, Camilla was admitted into the partnership. It was agreed that she paid £75000 into the business bank account as her capital and share of the goodwill. The partners decided that £50000 of Camilla's capital would be used to repay part of the mortgage.

It was agreed that the assets of the business be valued at:

	£
Premises	250000
Machinery	45000
Vehicles	65000
Inventory	10500
Trade receivables	19500
Goodwill	60000

It was agreed that in future profits and losses be shared in the ratio 3:2:1 respectively and that the 'new' partnership would have total capital of £240 000 provided by the partners in their profit-sharing ratios, the partners either withdrawing capital or introducing capital to achieve this.

It was further agreed that goodwill would not remain in the partnership books of account, any adjustments being made through the partners' capital accounts.

REQUIRED

(a) Prepare partners' capital accounts after the introduction of Camilla as a partner.   (12 marks)

(b) Prepare a statement of financial position at 30 November 2012 after the admission
   of Camilla as a partner.   (18 marks)

plus 2 marks for quality of written communication

ⓔ This is a complex question that tests your ability to distinguish between transactions that affect partners' capital accounts and those that affect partners' current accounts. It tests your ability to revalue the business assets where necessary. It also tests your ability to introduce and write off the intangible asset of goodwill in a partnership's books of account.

Student A

(a)   **Partners' capital accounts after admission of Camilla**

	A	B	C		A	B	C
Goodwill	30 000	20 000	10 000 ✓	Bal b/d	100 000	80 000 ✓	
Losses				Cash			75 000 ✓
Machinery	12 500	12 500		Premises	20 000	20 000	
Vehicle	7 500	7 500		Goodwill	30 000	30 000 ✓✓✓	
Inventory	750	750		Bank	21 000 ✓		
Tr rec'bles	250	250					
Bank		9 000 ✓	25 000 ✓				
Bal c/d	12 000	80 000	40 000 ✓				
	171 000	130 000	75 00		171 000	130 000	75 000
				Bal b/d	120 000	80 000	40 000 ✓

ⓔ **12/12 marks awarded** This is an excellent answer. There is a good heading and all the components are labelled clearly. However, student A has treated each of the adjustments to the assets as individual items. While this is not incorrect, it does take up valuable time. It is probably safer and less time-consuming to group all the changes to the asset values in one revaluation account and divide the profit (or loss) in the appropriate ratios. In this case, the profit on revaluation is £58 000, which would be shared between the two partners equally (£29 000 each).

(b) **Partnership statement of financial position at 30 November 2012 after the admission of Camilla as a partner**

	£	£
Non-current assets		
Premises		250 000 ✓
Machinery		45 000 ✓
Vehicle		65 000 ✓
		360 000
Non-current assets		
Inventory	10 500 ✓	
Trade receivables	19 500 ✓	
Bank (8000) + 75 000 – (9000)	4 000 ✓ ✓ ✓ ✓ ✓ ✓	
(25 000) + 21 000 – (50 000)	34 000	
Current liabilities		
Trade payables	(9 000) ✓	25 000
Non-current liabilities		
Mortgage		(140 000) ✓
		245 000
Capital accounts – Albert		120 000 ✓
Bertoli		80 000 ✓
Camilla		40 000 ✓
Current accounts – Albert		6 000
Bertoli		(1 000) ✓
		245 000

ⓔ **20/20 marks awarded** This is a well-presented answer that scores the full 18 marks for content. The heading and subheadings are perfect and so gain the 2 presentation marks available. The layout, showing subtotals, is also perfect. This is the script of a well-prepared student who has left nothing to chance. The bank balance is supported by accurate, detailed workings that would have scored part marks if the total had been incorrect.

ⓔ **Total: 32/32 marks awarded (grade A)**

Student B

(a)

Capital

	A	B	C		A	B	C
Goodwill	20 000	20 000	20 000	Bal	100 000	80 000 ✓	75 000
Bal	203 333	183 333	103 333	Goodwill	20 000	20 000	20 000
				Profit	103 333	103 333	103 333
	223 333	203 333	123 333		223 333	203 333	198 333
				Bal	203 333	183 333	103 333 ✓*

e **2/12 marks awarded** This is a poor effort. The capital introduced by Camilla is labelled balance rather than bank; the amount should have been shown separately from the opening balances. Camilla has been credited with part of the profits and goodwill that accrued before she became a partner; both should have been credited to the two original partners. The goodwill has been written off incorrectly. Student B has not followed the instructions in the question regarding the closing capital account balances; they do not add to £240000, nor are they shown in the profit-sharing ratios. However, by use of the student's own figures, the balances have been brought down correctly. This part of the answer is not worthy of a pass grade.

(b)

Financial position

Premises	250000 ✓
Machinery	45000 ✓
Vehicles	65000 ✓
Inventory	10500 ✓
Receivables	19500 ✓
Bank	67000
Payables	(9000) ✓
Mortgage	(190000)
	258000
Capitals	
Albert	203333 ✓*
Bertoli	183333 ✓*
Camilla	103333 ✓*
	489999

Sorry Mr Examiner, it doesn't balance I've made a mistake somewhere.

e **9/20 marks awarded** Student B has made a slightly better attempt at this part of the question than part (a). However, there are two careless errors in the use of £190000 for the mortgage and the complete omission of the current account balances. This has cost the student 2 valuable marks. A further 3 marks are forfeited by the lack of workings showing how the student has arrived at the bank balance.

No marks are awarded for presentation; the heading is incomplete and there are no subheadings for non-current assets, current assets etc. The student's message to the examiner is irrelevant and simply wastes time.

Had the simple basics been adhered to, Student B would have gained a pass grade but as it is, scores 9 marks out of a possible 20.

e **Total: 11/32 marks (fail)**

Question 5 **Financial statements of partnerships 2**

Ferdinand, Gerrard and Heskey have been in partnership for many years, sharing profits and losses in the ratio 3:2:1 respectively. They decide to dissolve the partnership with effect from the close of business on 30 November 2012.

They provide the following information:

Statement of financial position at 30 November 2012

	£	£
Non-current assets		
Premises	100000	
Fixtures and fittings	35000	
Vehicles (3)	25000	160000
Current assets		
Inventory	10000	
Trade receivables	22500	
	32500	
Current liabilities		
Trade payables	(17600)	
Bank overdraft	(6400)	
	(24000)	
Net current assets		8500
		168500
Long-term loan – Gerrard		(30000)
		138500
Capital accounts		
Ferdinand		60000
Gerrard		40000
Heskey		38500
		138500

The premises and fixtures and fittings were sold to Serrot plc for £200000. The purchase consideration consisted of £50000 cash, £30000 5% debentures to be shared between the partners in their profit-sharing ratios, and 90000 ordinary shares of £1 each to be shared equally between the partners.

One vehicle was taken over by Ferdinand at an agreed value of £10000.

Another vehicle was taken over by Heskey at an agreed value of £8000.

The third vehicle was sold for £2500 cash.

The inventory realised £8500 cash.

Trade receivables paid £22100.

Trade payables allowed £200 cash discount.

Dissolution expenses amounted to £5130.

REQUIRED

Prepare:

(a) a realisation account   (13 marks)

(b) a bank account   (11 marks)

(c) partners' capital accounts   (11 marks)

ⓔ Another complex question, this time dealing with the dissolution of a partnership. The question involves the purchase of assets of a partnership by a limited company. The purchase consideration often causes problems for students in the allocation and value of any ordinary shares. It also requires you to sell some assets for cash and 'sell' others to the partners.

Student A

(a)

Realisation account

Disc alld	400 ✓	Disc rec	200 ✓
Prem & fixt	135 000 ✓✓	Serrot	200 000 ✓
Veh	25 000 ✓	Cap Fer car	10 000 ✓
Inv	10 000 ✓	Hes car	8 000 ✓
Expenses	5 130 ✓	Cash veh	2 500 ✓
Profit	53 670 ✓	Cash inv	8 500 ✓
	229 200		229 200

ⓔ **13/13 marks awarded** There are too many abbreviations here. This criticism apart, this is a good, accurate answer that scores maximum marks. The student clearly achieves a grade A for this part of the answer.

(b)

Bank account

Trade rec	22 100 ✓	Bal b/d	6 400 ✓
Serrot plc	50 000 ✓	Trade pay	17 400 ✓
Car	2 500 ✓	Costs	5 130 ✓
Inventory	8 500 ✓	Ferdinand	16 835 ✓*
		Gerrard	29 890 ✓*
		Heskey	7 445 ✓*
	83 100		83 100

ⓔ **10/11 marks awarded** This is a sound answer to the second part of the question. There is one error: the loan repayment should have been settled separately from the capital account balances (see part c) and credited directly to the bank account.

(c)

Capital accounts

Debs	15000	10000	5000 ✓	Balances	60000	40000	38500 ✓
Shares	30000	30000	30000	Loan		30000	
Goodwill	15000	10000	5000	Profit	26835 ✓	17890 ✓	8945 ✓
Cars	10000 ✓	8000 ✓					
Bank	16835	29890	7445				
	86835	87890	47445		86835	87890	47445

Workings

Serrots account

200000	Cash	50000	
	Debs	30000	
	Shs	90000	
	Goodwill	30000	

ⓔ **7/11 marks awarded** Student A has made a few basic errors. The loan account should not be credited to the capital account but should be paid directly out of the bank account to the former partner. In Serrot's account (workings), the shares have a value of £120000 (£90000 plus a share premium of £30000). The inclusion of the 'goodwill' has had serious consequences for the student; not only is the value placed on the shares incorrect but an extraneous item has been introduced into each partner's capital account, thus depriving the student of own figure marks for the cash balances to be paid to the partners. It was pleasing to note that the surplus funds in the bank account had not been split in the profit-sharing ratios but had been used to close the capital accounts.

ⓔ **Total: 30/35 marks (grade A)**

Student B

(a)

Realisation account

Disc alld	400 ✓	Disc rec	200 ✓
Receivables	22500	Payables	17400
Premises & fix	65000	Vehicles	4500
		Inventory	8500 ✓
		Goodwill	30000
		Loss	27300
	87900		87900

ⓔ **3/13 marks awarded** Student B has given a confused answer. Both trade receivables and trade payables have been included in the realisation account as well as the respective discounts. Although the profit on the disposal of the premises and fixtures has been calculated accurately, it has been entered on the wrong side of the realisation account. The loss on the disposal of the vehicles has also been accurately calculated and entered incorrectly. The premium on the shares has been included as goodwill and the dissolution expenses have not been included. There are too many basic errors here, errors that should not be made by an A2 student.

(b)

Bank account

Balance	6 400	Payables	400
Serrot	50 000 ✓	Ferdinand	36 165 ✓*
Car	2 500 ✓	Gerrard	24 110 ✓*
Inventory	8 500 ✓	Heskey	12 055 ✓*
Receivables	200		
Costs	5 130		
	72 730		72 730

ℯ **6/11 marks awarded** This is a much better attempt than in part (a) but there are still too many fundamental errors. The opening overdraft has been entered on the wrong side, as has the payment of the expenses of the dissolution. The discounts received and paid have been included rather than the cash paid and cash received. The closing bank balance has been divided incorrectly between the partners in their profit-sharing ratios. However, it has been rewarded since the bookkeeping has been performed correctly by debiting the amounts to the capital accounts.

(c)

Capital accounts

	F	G	H		F	G	H
Debs	15 000	10 000	5 000 ✓	Bal b/d	60 000	40 000	38 500 ✓
Shares	30 000	30 000	30 000	Goodwill	15 000	10 000	5 000
Loss	13 650 ✓*	9 100 ✓*	4 550 ✓*				
Cars	10 000 ✓	8 000 ✓					
Cash	36 165	24 110	12 055				

ℯ **7/11 marks awarded** Although there are a number of errors, student B has completed the double entry for the debentures, the loss (own figure) and the cars taken over by the respective partners. The opening balance is also correct. No attempt has been made to add the accounts because it is obvious that they will not balance. It is always useful to complete the accounts by adding them since, if you have made only a single error, the difference in the totals may reveal what the error is.

ℯ **Total: 16/35 marks (grade E)**

Question 6 **Published financial statements of limited companies I**

(a) Identify two interested parties in the financial statements of limited companies. Explain the reasons for their interest and the information they would seek. (6 marks)

(b) Explain two reasons why a limited company publishes its annual report and financial statements. (8 marks)

plus 2 marks for quality of written communication

(c) Discuss two limitations to interested parties of using the published accounts of limited companies. (10 marks)

ⓔ This is another complex question covering three related topics concerning the published financial statements of limited companies. It requires you to have a knowledge of the parties who might be interested in analysing the published statements and the reasons for their interest. You are also required to have a knowledge of the stewardship function of accounting and the limitations that are inherent in using the 'abridged' published versions of limited companies' financial statements.

Student A

(a) Investors. ✓ Is the business making a profit? ✓ Is it able to pay for its comitments? ✓ They are interested in this so that they can judge if the managers are up to the job. ✓ They are also interested to see if there is enough money to pay for the dividends. ✓   **max. 3 marks**
Managers. ✓ Is our company making a profit? ✓ How well are we using our resources? ✓ Is the company expanding or contracting? ✓ Is the company a going concern? ✓ So are our jobs safe? ✓   **max. 3 marks**

ⓔ **6/6 marks awarded** This is a sound answer. The interested parties have been identified and reasons for their interest have been given along with required information. The student has misspelled 'commitments' and there is use of colloquial English.

(b) The Companies Act 1985 as amended by the Companies Act 1989 set out the rules so limited companys are regulated by the two acts. All limited companys must keep the shareholders (i.e. the owners of the company) informed ✓ on how the company has performed during the year in question. ✓ This is part of the stewardship function of accountancy. ✓ This is because the shareholders apoint the directors to run the company on their behalf. Generally there are thousands of shareholders — they cannot all run the company so they apoint directors to do it for them. ✓ This is known as the divorce of ownership and control. ✓ **max. 4 marks**
   The accounts are published also to show people who might wish to invest in the company just how it is doing. ✓ They will want to see if it is making a profit ✓ and whether the profits are growing or shrinking. ✓ They will also want to see how big the dividend that they will get from their investment is ✓ and whether it is getting bigger each year. ✓   **max. 4 marks**

plus I mark for quality of written communication

e **9/10 marks awarded** This is another sound answer containing some good points. The student has identified the reasons and has then developed them. Only 1 mark is awarded for quality of written communication since there are several incorrect spellings.

(c) (1) The information shown is historical; they show financial facts that occurred during the last financial year. ✓ This does not necessarily mean that good things will be repeated in the future. ✓

(2) They only show things that can be measured in money terms. ✓ They cannot show if the work force is unhappy or exploited. ✓

My conclusion is that despite the limitations, the amount of information made available to interested parties more than makes up for the limitations identified above. ✓

e **5/10 marks awarded** Both limitations identified in this answer would have benefited from further development. For example, reference to more years' figures can determine trends in order to give more idea of what might reasonably be expected to happen in the future. The second point could have discussed the effects of motivation, such as labour turnover or any potential improvement in the figures if the workforce was to become more motivated.

It was good to see that the student recognised the need for a judgement to be made, as indicated by the use of the trigger word 'discuss' in the question.

e **Total: 20/26 marks (grade A)**

Student B

(a) Employees ✓ are interested. Has the company made a profit ✓ because that will make jobs safe? ✓   **3 marks**

Suppliers ✓ are interested. Has the company enough money to pay us? ✓ Is it making a profit because profits are necessary for the long-term survival of the business and we would like to continue to supply them in the future. ✓   **3 marks**

e **6/6 marks awarded** There is just enough detail here to score all the available marks.

(b) I am going to explain to you two reasons why a public limited company publishes its annual report and financial statements. First of all they have to because the government says they must. They prepare the accounts then send them to shareholders and to Companies House to be filed. ✓ They send them to the shareholders so that they know how the company is doing. ✓ The shareholders get a vote at the AGM and if they don't like what they have read in the accounts they can vote off the directors. ✓   **3 marks**

Secondly the government can see the accounts and can see whether the company has paid the right amount of tax. If not they can be fined.

plus 1 mark for quality of written communication

e **4/10 marks awarded** The first sentence is superfluous and costs the student valuable time. Overall this is a rather weak answer. The first reason could have been developed to include stewardship. Although the language used is simplistic and the answer should contain more technical language, it has been awarded 1 mark for quality of communication.

(c) The published accounts are in an abridged form ✓ so they don't show the full picture. They are hard to understand.

e **1/10 marks awarded** This answer is too short. There are 10 marks available and an answer that comprises only 20 words cannot possibly score a respectable number of marks — more detail and development is necessary. Limitations can never include that something is hard to do.

e **Total: 11/26 marks awarded (grade E)**

Question 7 Published financial statements of limited companies 2

Evaluate the usefulness to the users of financial statements of each of the following:

(a) notes to the financial statements (8 marks)

(b) the directors' report (8 marks)

(c) the auditors' report (7 marks)

plus 2 marks for quality of written communication

ⓔ This question requires you to have a more detailed knowledge of parts of the published financial statements of limited companies and the usefulness of such information to the many users of accounting information. Remember that it is always a good idea to use a plan when answering a written question. The 'quality' marks require you to concentrate on the spellings and grammar that you use. These marks can move you up into a higher grade boundary.

Student A

(a) IAS 7 states that notes are to be included as part of the financial statements. ✓ The complete set is made up of:
- an income statement for the year
- a statement of financial position for the year
- a statement of cash flows
- a statement of changes to equity
- notes to explain some of the information and to outline accounting policies
  The notes give information on how the financial statements have been compiled. ✓
  The notes should disclose information required by the standards that is not shown in the financial statement. ✓ The information is designed to make the financial statements more understandable to the users. ✓
  The notes cover items like:
- a statement to say that the appropriate standards have been followed
- a summary of significant accounting policies followed. The company will generally say that the accounts have been prepared using historical cost in the main with perhaps some revaluations. **Max 2 marks for examples**
  The notes will also detail supporting information ✓ for items in all the financial statements. It will show much of the detail that will help the users of the financial statements to understand what the figures contain, for example how the tax bill on the income statement is made up; a schedule of non-current assets showing the property, plant and equipment; and the changes during the year. It also gives details of how each item shown in total on the statement of financial position is composed.
  How the share capital is made up is also shown in the notes. **Max 2 marks for examples**

The notes have to show the amounts of dividends paid to shareholders and how much this is per share. They must also state the amount of proposed dividends declared. This does not appear in the financial statements because they may not be agreed by the shareholders at the AGM. ✓

My judgement is that the notes are essential to help the shareholders and other stakeholders understand the details of what is in the statements because the actual statements themselves are basically summaries (like a skeleton) leaving out most of the detail.

2 marks

ⓔ **8/8 marks awarded** Student A has made 12 mark-worthy points but is limited to 8 marks. This is a comprehensive answer with good use of examples as part of the development. The student has given a good judgement.

(b) The directors must prepare a report on the year. This is part of the Companies Act 1985. ✓ It gives all their names and how many shares in the company they own. It also gives their remuneration and pension rights. The report must show a statement of what the company does — that is, its principal trading activities; ✓ it gives a review of how the company has performed over the past year ✓ — that is, all the good things and bad things that the company has done during the year. It also shows any big movements in non-current assets over the year, ✓ the company's policy on employing people with disabilities and the company's policy on health and safety at work; on getting employees involved in determining company decisions; the payment of suppliers; who and how much they have given to political parties; how much dividend they propose to pay out.

2 marks for examples

My judgement is that the directors' report is useful because it backs up the information given in the financial statements. ✓ Once again it provides details basically of why the business has behaved as it has. ✓

ⓔ **8/8 marks awarded** This answer makes good use of examples and again a pleasing judgement is made.

(c) The auditors made sure that the financial statements give a true and fair view of what has happened in the company over the year. ✓ The shareholders appoint the auditors to report to them. ✓ The auditors are qualified accountants so they know what they are looking for. After examining the financial statements they give their opinion ✓ on whether the financial statements have been prepared accurately.

My judgement is that is it essential to have an 'outsider' look at the financial statements ✓ to state whether they are correct and whether any of the directors are covering up anything. ✓

ⓔ **7/9 marks awarded** Student A scores 5 marks for content. The student could have discussed the parts of the report and commented on the two types of opinion that could be given. However, despite these minor criticisms this is a well-thought-out and presented answer that also gains 2 marks for quality of written communication.

ⓔ **Total: 23/25 marks (grade A)**

Student B

(a) The law states that all financial statements should contain notes to the accounts. The financial statements that are filed at Companies House and are sent to all the shareholders are an abridged version of the financial statements that the company uses inside the company. ✓ The notes give more details and explanations as to how the figures are made up. ✓

    The notes are useful ✓ otherwise they would not be included.

@ **3/8 marks awarded** This is a limited answer that would have benefited from much more detail and development. The student did give a judgement but the justification was inappropriate.

(b) Directors are the owners of the company and it is up to them to tell the shareholders who have provided the money for the company what has happened to the money (this is called stewardship). ✓

    Their report tells us how the figures in the income statement and the SOFP and the statement of cash flows are made up. ✓

    The directors' report is not very useful because it simply repeats the information given in the notes to the statements.

@ **2/8 marks awarded** This is a poor response. Shareholders are the owners; directors are employees, of the company. They are appointed by the shareholders and should work for the benefit of the shareholders. Once more, little detail and development is offered. The judgement is poor. The directors' report gives details of the bases and policies used to arrive at the figures detailed in the statements.

(c) The auditors work for the shareholders. ✓ They check that the people inside the company have not been on the fiddle.

    The report has three sections:
    (1) What their responsibilities are and what the directors' responsibilities are. ✓
    (2) The basis of opinion — what the auditors did to check the books of account. ✓
    (3) Their opinion as to whether the accounts give a true and fair view of what has gone on in the company. ✓

    If they don't think that everything is above board then they should say this in their report — this is called a qualified report ✓. It is very bad if a company gets a qualified report and it will affect the share price on the stock exchange.

    It is essential that there is a report from the auditors ✓ otherwise how do we know whether the financial statements are correct? ✓

@ **7/9 marks awarded** This is a much better answer. The student has obviously learned what auditors do and what their report contains. Although this is not a perfect response, there is sufficient evidence that the student understands the role of the auditors.

@ **Total: 12/25 marks (grade E)**

Question 8 **Accounting standards 1: statements of cash flows**

The following statements of financial position and notes to the accounts are given for Stangrit plc:

Statements of financial position at 31 December

	£000	2012 £000	£000	2011 £000
Non-current assets (note 1)		3 228		1 825
Current assets				
Inventory	570		634	
Trade receivable	1 161		946	
Cash and cash equivalents	61		41	
	1 792		1 621	
Current liabilities				
Trade payable	(937)		(846)	
Tax	(220)		(130)	
	(1 157)		(976)	
Net current assets		635		645
		3 863		2 470
Non-current liabilities				
8% debentures (note 2)		(1 000)		(500)
		2 863		1 970
Equity				
Ordinary shares of £1 each (note 3)		1 000		500
Share premium account		—		200
Retained earnings		1 863		1 270
		2 863		1 970

Statement of changes in equity

	Equity £000	Share premium £000	Revaluation reserve £000	Retained earnings £000
Balance at 1 January 2012	500	200	–	1 270
Profit for the year	–	–	–	853
Dividends paid	–	–	–	(210)
Revaluation of land and buildings	–	–	250	–
Issue of bonus shares	500	(200)	(250)	(50)
Balance at 31 December 2012	1 000	–	–	1 863

Extract from income statement for the year ended 31 December 2012

	£000
Profit from operations	1 048
Finance expense	(60)
Finance income	85
Profit before tax	1 073
Tax	(220)
Profit for the year	853

	31 December 2012	31 December 2011
	£000	£000
Land and buildings		
Cost	–	600
Valuation	700	–
Aggregate depreciation	(14)	(150)
Carrying amount	686	450

During the year ended 31 December 2012 the land and buildings were revalued at £700 000. There were no disposals of land and buildings during the year.

Plant and machinery		
Cost	350	350
Additions during the year	175	–
Disposals	(115)	–
Aggregate depreciation to date	(143)	(210)
Carrying amount	267	140

During the year ended 31 December 2012 a machine that had cost £115 000 was sold at a profit of £10 000. The machine had been depreciated by £108 000 up to the date of its disposal. Machinery costing £175 000 was acquired during the year. Plant and machinery are depreciated at 10% per annum on cost.

Vehicles		
Cost	140	140
Additions during the year	100	–
Aggregate depreciation	(165)	(105)
Carrying amount	75	35

There were no disposals of vehicles during the year.

Long-term investments		
Cost	2 200	1 200

There were no disposals of investments during the year.

REQUIRED

(a) Prepare a statement of cash flows for the year ended 31 December 2012.

   (A statement showing reconciliation of net cash flow to movement in net debt is not required.) (23 marks)

   plus 2 marks for quality of presentation

(b) Explain how the following should be treated in a statement of cash flows:
   (i) depreciation
   (ii) profit on sale of machinery (4 marks)

A junior clerk was heard to remark, 'I do not know why the finance director prepares a statement of cash flows. She has produced an income statement and a statement of financial position, surely that must be sufficient information?'

REQUIRED

(c) Draft a memorandum addressed to the clerk explaining why the finance director produces a statement of cash flows each financial year.

(9 marks)

plus 2 marks for quality of written communication

ⓔ This is a detailed, comprehensive question on the preparation of a statement of cash flows. It includes all the 'tricky' changes that could take place during a financial year, including the revaluation of non-current assets, the issue of bonus shares and the disposal and acquisition of non-current assets. The key to success is to tackle this type of question in a methodical, meticulous way. Remember that, when you use workings, don't just key them into your calculator; show the details in your answer book.

Student A

(a)

Workings

Money in		Money out	
Depn add to profit	41	PM bought	175
Disp M	17	Take off profit	10
Depn V	60	Vehicle bought	100
Depn LB	14	Inv bought	1 000
Profit	1 048	Int paid	60
Int rec	85	TR up	215
Inv inc	64	Tax pd	130
TP up	91	Div pd	210
Deb issue	500		1 900
	1 920		

Statement of cash flows at 31 December 2012

	£000	£000
Operating profit		1 048 ✓
Depreciation		115 ✓✓✓
Profit on disposal		(10) ✓
Decrease in inventories		64 ✓
Increase in trade receivables		(215) ✓
Increase in trade payable		91 ✓
Cash from operating activities		1 093 ✓
Interest paid		(60) ✓
Interest received		85
Income tax paid		(220)
Cash from operating activities		898

Investing activities		
Purchase of machine	(175) ✓	
Vehicles	(100) ✓	
Cash from the sale of machine	17 ✓	
Cash spent on investing activities		(258) ✓
Financing activities		
Money from debenture issue	500 ✓	
Purchase of investments	(1 000)	
Dividends paid	(210) ✓	
Cash spent on financing		(710)
Increase in cash and cash equivalents		20 ✓
Cash and cash equivalents at start of year		41 ✓
Cash and cash equivalents at end of year		61 ✓

ⓔ **20/25 marks awarded** Student A scores 19 marks plus 1 mark for presentation (the heading mark was not awarded — the statement is prepared for a year not one day). The layout is very good. The only errors are that interest received should be under the financing activities section and the investments purchased should be classified as an investing activity. The student has used this year's provision rather than the actual tax paid. Only 1 mark was awarded for the increase of £20000 in cash and cash equivalents, although 2 marks were available. The student clearly knew that this was the increase during the year and was rewarded for this. However, the statement does not add to this, hence the penalty. These are minor errors in such a detailed question.

> **(b)** Depreciation is a non-cash expense. ✓ It reduces the profit but it does
> not use cash so it has to be added back to the profit to get the true
> cash figure. ✓   **2 marks**
>   Profit on sale of the machinery is a 'book entry'. It increases
> profits but not cash. ✓ The actual cash income was £17000. ✓   **2 marks**

ⓔ **4/4 marks awarded** These are good, concise answers. The student has matched the length of answer to the number of marks given.

> **(c)** To: Junior clerk   MEMORANDUM   Date: 15 January 2012
> From: Tom Smith
> Subject: Reasons for preparation of a statement of cash flows
> Dear junior clerk
> The company prepares a statement of cash flows because IAS 7 requires that
> limited companies do ✓ as part of the stewardship function of accounting. ✓
> Businesses require good cash flows because cash is so important for short-term
> survival. ✓ Someone once said 'It is the life blood of the business'. So the standard
> concentrates on cash inflows and outflows. ✓ The statement reveals information
> that isn't shown on the income statement. ✓ It lets users of the statements see
> how effectively the business is raising cash during the year and how wisely it
> is spending it ✓ (stewardship). The business has raised money through issuing
> debentures and has spent it on assets and the purchase of investments. ✓ It
> allows us to see the changes in all the assets and liabilities during the year.

(e) **9/11 marks awarded** This is a well-written answer, although a memorandum should never start with 'Dear…'. The student could have mentioned the use of statements of cash flows for comparative purposes and that the statement highlights the internal and external cash inflows and outflows. Otherwise, this is a commendable effort, gaining 2 marks for quality of written communication.

(e) **Total: 33/40 marks (grade A)**

Student B

(a) Stangrit plc. Statement of cash flows for the year ended 31 December 2012

Operating profit	1 048 ✓	
Depreciation	(115)	
Profit on disposal	10	
Decrease in inventory	64 ✓	Ostriches
Increase in trade receivables	(215) ✓	Invade
Increase in trade payables	91 ✓	France
Interest paid	(60) ✓	
Interest received	85	
Tax paid	(130) ✓	
Investments		
Purchases of non-current assets	(1 403)	
Sales of non-current assets	17 ✓	
Financing		
Sale of debentures	500 ✓	
Dividends paid	(210) ✓	
Decrease in cash	(385)	
Cash at start of year	41 ✓	
Decrease in cash	(385)	
Cash at end of year	(344)	should be 61

(e) **11/25 marks awarded** This is a reasonable attempt but the student has made too many errors. One mark was awarded for quality of presentation for the heading. The subheadings are all there in a shortened form (aided by the use of a good mnemonic).

The major errors are that the depreciation charge and profit on disposal are both in the wrong 'direction' and an incorrect figure is used for purchases of non-current assets. We also have another example of a student writing superfluous comments ('should be 61') that simply waste time and effort.

(b) Depreciation is a non-cash expense ✓ and so should go in the income statement. It is also cash put away so that new assets can be bought in the future so it is taken away.   **1 mark**
    Profit on disposal is good. It increases the bank balance and also increases the profit so it is added.

e 1/4 marks awarded This is a poor effort for an A2 student. The non-cash expense is the only redeeming feature of this section but the student contradicts this statement by stating that cash is put away for future use. The comment regarding the profit on disposal indicates that the student does not understand the difference between cash and profits.

(c) Dear Junior clerk

The cash flow statement provides a link between the two statements of financial position ✓ and it shows cash inflows and outflows ✓ like money spent buying investments and money paid to debentures. ✓ It can be used to show the bank manager how you will spend money in the future if you want to borrow money from him. It will also tell you if you have too much money then you can even buy more investments.

If I can be of any further assistance to you do not hesitate to call me at work or on my mobile.

Yours etc.

Raymond Jones (Accountant)

e 3/11 marks awarded This is a poor attempt at producing a memorandum. The heading is missing the important details. The student has wasted more time with an ending that is not at all business-like. There is one good point and it is well developed with the use of examples.

e 15/40 marks awarded (fail)

Question 9 Accounting standards 2

The finance director of Bandshield plc has prepared a draft set of financial statements. He has calculated the profit for the year at £5 453 860.

However, the following items were not taken into account when a draft income statement for the year ended 31 December 2012 was prepared:

(1) The inventory at 31 December 2012 had been valued at cost. One group of inventories had been damaged; they had cost £720 and would normally have sold for £1080. In order to sell these goods, repairs were undertaken. Advertisements to sell the goods were made on the internet and in local newspapers and the goods were sold on 4 January 2013 for £800. The advertisements cost £85 and the repairs cost £105.

(2) The directors had proposed a final dividend of £75 000. This will be paid in April 2013. This had not been included in any of the financial statements.

(3) Property, plant and equipment has been entered in the statement of financial position at 31 December 2012 at a carrying amount of £1 200 000. The fair value of the assets less costs to sell is £800 000. The present value in use is estimated to be £1 000 000.

(4) In November 2012 the directors introduced a new product and named it 'Branspear'. They believe that this brand name is probably worth £10 000 000. They have included it as an intangible non-current asset on the statement of financial position at 31 December 2012 and have amortised it at 10% since that is the annual depreciation charge on the company's other non-current assets. The carrying amount shown on the statement of financial position for the brand name is £9 000 000.

REQUIRED

(a) Prepare a statement showing the correct profit for the year. (5 marks)

(b) Explain your treatment of each of the items (1)–(4), making reference to any International Accounting Standards (IAS) that apply. (20 marks)

ⓔ International accounting standards set the ground rules of how accounting standards should be applied to everyday accounting situations. This question deals with four common problems requiring you to apply the appropriate standard encountered in your studies to the way they influence reported profits.

You must have a knowledge of the international standards and their application to answer part (b) of the question. Do remember to identify any transaction(s) that has no effect on your answer — the examiner must know that you have not missed it (them) out because you did not know how to deal with it.

Student A

(a)

Statement correcting the profit

£

Original profit	5 453 860
1 Inventory	(110) ✓
2 Proposed dividend	no entry ✓
3 PPE	(200 000) ✓
4 Brand name	1 000 000 ✓
Correct profit	6 253 750 ✓

ⓔ **5/5 marks awarded** This is a perfect answer. Each adjustment to the profit is labelled and numbered and there is a clear, concise heading. Student A has made it clear that the proposed dividend did not adjust the profit. Some students do not do this, but merely miss out the offending adjustment — the examiner will not award a mark in such cases as it is impossible to know whether the student knows the treatment or whether it has been omitted through lack of knowledge.

(b) (1) Inventories of all kinds must be valued at cost or net realisable value, whichever is the lowest. ✓ This is stated in IAS 1 Inventories. ✓ The finance director knows this because the goods were sold just after the year end. Also this is an adjusting event ✓ because the knowledge was gained, I think, before the financial statements were authorised for publication. ✓ The cost of the goods was £720 and the net realisable value was £610 ✓ (the sale price less all the costs getting them ready for sale £85 and £105 ✓) so £610 must be chosen as it is lower than £720. **max. 5 marks**

(2) Proposed dividends are not included in the financial statements ✓ because the shareholders might reject that amount when they meet at the company's AGM ✓ (they can pull the dividend down but they cannot put it up). Last year's proposed dividend will be included in this year's financial statements because it will have been paid in this financial year. ✓ This is part of the prudence concept. **3 marks**

ⓔ Student A is correct to omit the proposed dividend since it is a non-adjusting event. They are not liabilities at the end of the reporting period since the condition arose after the reporting period, i.e. in April 2013. The standard to be applied is IAS 10, Events after the reporting period. The proposed dividend should be detailed in the notes to the financial statements.

(3) The property, plant and equipment has been impaired. ✓ IAS 36 impairment of assets ✓ says that if the value of an asset shown on the statement of financial position (this is called the carrying amount) is bigger than what the asset could be sold for or how much it could earn for the company, then it has been impaired. ✓ In this case the statement of financial position value is greater than either the selling price £800 000 and the future incomes generated £1 000 000. ✓ (These incomes have to be discounted to give a net present value.) I have chosen the future incomes because this gives a truer value of the assets. ✓ £200 000 needs to be taken from the profits — impairment is rather like the depreciation expense (a non-cash expense) ✓ **max. 5 marks**

ⓔ The English is a little clumsy but this is a good answer. The student clearly knows the essential elements of IAS 36.

> (4) IAS 38 deals with intangible assets. ✓ A brand name is an intangible asset. It is 'an identifiable asset without physical substance'. ✓ IAS 38 states that internally generated brand names (and internally generated goodwill) cannot be classed as an asset of the company. ✓ If the name had been bought from another company this treatment would have been acceptable. ✓ **4 marks**

ⓔ **17/20 marks awarded** This is a sound answer. More marks could have been earned with some development: for example, reference to the amortisation and its treatment. The student could have questioned whether the company would have benefited from the brand name in the future and if any future benefits could be measured reliably.

ⓔ **Total: 22/25 marks (grade A)**

Student B

(a)	5 453 860
I can't do — the value of inventory used isn't given in the question so not possible	
2	(75 000)
3	(400 000)
4	**correct so leave it**
Profit	4 978 000 ✓*

ⓔ **1/5 marks awarded** This is a poor effort. The statement lacks a heading and descriptions of the various adjustments. The comments are superfluous and simply waste time. The student does not realise the basic fact that any change in the valuation of inventories affects profits by the amount of the change. The finance director correctly omitted the proposed dividends since they are a non-adjusting event. Although the student used the right principle in item 3, the amount chosen was incorrect. The amount chosen should be the recoverable amount, which is the larger of the fair value (£800 000) and the value in use (£1 000 000). Since this is greater than the carrying amount, the assets have been impaired by £200 000. Carrying amount £1 200 000 less £1 000 000 = £200 000. Internally generated brand names cannot be recognised as assets.

> **(b)** The inventory should be valued at the lower of cost and net realisable value. ✓ This is part of IAS 2 Inventories. ✓
>   Cost is £720 + £85 and £105 so the goods have cost £905. The NRV is £1080 so I would have used £905 because it's the lowest but I don't know what the total cost for inventories was. **2 marks**

ⓔ The overriding principle to be used in the valuation of inventories has been identified. The standard has also been recognised. However, the principle was not applied. Net realisable value is selling price less any costs incurred to make the sale, so net realisable value in this case is £610 (£800 − £85 − £105). This is a common error made each year by many students.

Proposed dividends are owed at the end of the year so they need to be taken off the profit in a statement of equity along with the interim dividend paid during the year. This is IAS 1 Accruals.

ⓔ Proposed dividends are non-adjusting events (IAS 10) and should not be included in the body of the financial statements. They should be shown as a note to the financial statements.

Assets should be valued at the lower of cost and net realisable value. NRV is the selling price so £800 000 should be used as this is what they could be sold for. The assets are overvalued by £400 000. This is the amount of the impairment £400 000. ✓* It is IAS 36 impairment of assets. ✓   **2 marks**

ⓔ The standard has been correctly identified. The student has used the lower of fair value and value in use rather than the higher of the two figures.

A brand name is an intangible asset so IAS 38 intangible assets ✓ applies here. Amortisation is the term used when intangible assets are depreciated. It is reasonable to depreciate the brand name by 10% if that is the amount that the other assets are depreciated. This money should be put away so that new assets and new brand names can be purchased in the future.   **I mark**

ⓔ **5/20 marks awarded** After recognising the correct standard, Student B goes off at a tangent and discusses depreciation, under the misapprehension that depreciation provides a cache of liquid funds that can be used to purchase further assets in the future. Student B seems to be unaware that depreciation is a book entry only.

Student B has clearly made an effort to learn the number and heading of the standards and can recognise the scenarios that the standard would influence, but needs to spend more time revising the general principles covered by each of the standards that may be examined.

ⓔ **Total: 6/25 marks (fail)**

Question 10 **Valuation of inventory**

Tan Lian is in business; her year end is 30 September 2012. She values her inventory using the periodic method. Tan was ill in September and could not carry out her end-of-year inventory valuation.

On 10 October her inventory was valued at £7963.

Her accountant has prepared a draft set of financial statements using an estimated inventory valuation of £8200. Using this valuation he has calculated Tan's profit to be £26 780.

The following transactions took place in the period 1 to 9 October:

	£
Sales invoiced to customers	952
Purchases of goods for resale	504
Goods returned by customers, originally sold for	119
Goods returned to suppliers	84
Goods taken for own use at cost price	420

Tan marks up her goods uniformly by 40% on cost.

Additional information:

(1) Included in the inventory valuation were goods Tan had acquired for £882 on a sale or return basis. She had not yet decided whether to purchase the goods or return them.

(2) Included in the inventory were goods that had cost £400. The goods had been damaged during September and were to be sold for £380. However, repairs costing £60 would have to be completed before the goods could be sold.

(3) Goods sold during September were awaiting collection by the customer. The goods had been included in the inventory at their selling price of £140.

REQUIRED

(a) Calculate the correct value of inventory at 30 September 2012.   (19 marks)

(b) Explain your treatment of the items of additional information.   (8 marks)

(c) Calculate a corrected profit or loss for the year ended 30 September 2012.   (5 marks)

(d) Explain what is meant by a 'periodic' method of inventory valuation.   (3 marks)

@ Inventory valuation influences reported profits. This question deals with a 'real life' situation where valuation does not take place at the close of business on the final day of the financial year.

It tests your ability to understand the difference between 'mark-up' and 'margin' and its effect on the sales that have taken place after the year end.

The question also tests your understanding of 'periodic' and 'perpetual' methods of inventory valuation.

Student A

(a)   **Calculation of correct inventory valuation at 30 September 2012** ✓

	£
Inventory at 10 October 2012	7963 ✓
Sales	680 ✓ ✓ ✓
Purchases	(504) ✓
Sales returns	(85) ✓ ✓ ✓
Purchases returns	84 ✓
Goods for own use	(420)
Sale or return goods	(882) ✓
Damaged goods	(80) ✓✓ ✓ ✓
Goods not collected	(100)
Correct inventory	6656 ✓*

ⓔ **16/19 marks awarded** Student A has used a clear heading and comprehensive descriptions for each adjustment. This is a sound answer, but the student has not shown any workings to back up the figures.

It cannot be stressed too strongly that workings should always be shown, even for what might appear to be a very simple calculation. Even a calculation that has been completed successfully dozens of times in class and/or for homework is sometimes miscalculated. Examiners are constantly amazed to note how even the brightest students can make simple errors under the pressures of the examination.

(b) Explanation 1. I have taken away £882 because the goods still belong to the seller even though Tan has got them. Tan is being used just like another warehouse in which the seller's goods are being stored. ✓   **1 mark**

ⓔ This is a comprehensive answer. The student has clearly indicated which item is being discussed.

Explanation 2. Inventories must always be valued at the lower of cost or net realisable value ✓. The goods cost £400 plus the repair costs so altogether they cost £460. They should be valued at £380, which is £80 more than what they are included at, so I took this off. ✓   **2 marks**

ⓔ Student A scores 1 mark for recognising that inventories are always valued at the lower of cost and net realisable value; the second mark is awarded for choosing £380 (the student's own net realisable value) rather than £460 (student's own cost figure).

Explanation 3. These goods should not be included. ✓ They belong to the customer so I took £100 away. £100 is the cost price if the selling price is £140.   **1 mark**

ⓔ **4/8 marks awarded** The student has identified that the goods belong to the customer but has incorrectly taken off the mark-up to arrive at the valuation.

(c)

8200 ✓ − 6656 ✓* = 1544

Accountant's wrong profit	£26 780 ✓
Less decrease in inventory	1 544 ✓*
Correct profit figure	£25 236 ✓*

ⓔ **5/5 marks awarded** This is an accurate answer using the student's own figures.

(d) A periodic method of valuing inventory means that the inventory is valued only once rather than on a continuous basis ✓ — generally at the end of the year end. ✓ It is the method that is generally used by small businesses that do not have IT machines at the check out. ✓ The other type is perpetual. **3 marks**

ⓔ **3/3 marks awarded** Although the answer is not expressed very well, the student clearly understands the principle involved in a periodic valuation.

ⓔ **Total: 28/35 marks (grade A)**

Student B

(a)

	£
	8200
Sales 952 ✓ × 40%	380.8 ✓
Purchases 504 × 40%	201.60
Sales rets 119 ✓ × 40% ✓*	(47.60) ✓
Purchases rets 84 × 40%	33.60
Own use	(420)
SOR	882
Goods	(80) ✓✓ ✓ ✓ 400 − 320
Customers goods	(56) 140 × 40%
	12 093.20

ⓔ **9/19 marks awarded** This is a rather a messy attempt. However, on a positive note, the student has shown workings for all the adjustments, scoring 3 marks that would not have been gained if no workings had been evident.

There is no heading to indicate what the student is attempting. Student B has used the accountant's inventory valuation, not the value taken on 10 October. The figures are not aligned, which can make adding the columns difficult. Some items have pence, others show only pounds, which could result in errors being made. The student seems to be uncertain which items need adjusting to take into account the 40% mark-up; even then, 40% has been used rather than 100/140ths.

AQA A2 Accounting

The student's own corrected total of the inventory should have been £9094.40, which would have scored a mark.

(b) (1) These goods still belong to Tan. The customer has not yet told Tan if they want the goods or not.   **0 marks**

ⓔ Student B has misread the question. Always read questions slowly and carefully. Scan reading can often result in the facts being confused.

(2) I have taken 80 away to get the correct answer. ✓   **I mark**

ⓔ This answer does not explain why the student has used £80. The whole process should have been explained. Why did the student use £80? Were any concepts involved in the decision?

(3) The goods don't belong to Tan — she needs to take them off. ✓   **I mark**

ⓔ **2/8 marks awarded** Although the explanation is a little brief it scores a mark.

(c)

Sales		380.80
Sales rets		47.60
		333.20
Inventory	8200.00	
Purchases	201.60	
	8401.60	
Inventory	12093.20	3691.60
Gross loss		3358.40

I've made a mistake somewhere

ⓔ **0/5 marks awarded** Student B has adopted the wrong approach by trying to prepare the trading section of an income statement. This has resulted in a confused attempt. The student has made a superfluous comment at the end of the attempt. No marks are scored.

(d) There are lots of methods of valuing inventory. Periodic is one, AVCO is the other. With periodic the ones bought at the start are the ones to be sold first. It is the easiest one to do, which is why the tax people like it.

ⓔ **0/3 marks awarded** This is a very confused attempt. The student has written the odd word remembered from lessons (or revision) on inventory valuation. There is nothing of value in this attempt.

ⓔ **Total: 11/35 marks (fail)**

Knowledge check answers

1 A bank loan is finance borrowed from a bank. Interest has to be paid. It is generally medium- to long-term finance for a specific project. It is usually shown on a statement of financial position as a non-current asset. A bank overdraft shows that a business has drawn cheques on an account that had insufficient funds to cover the withdrawal. An arranged overdraft usually incurs lower interest charges than one that is not agreed beforehand. It is generally a short-term (current) liability.

2 Ordinary shares are the most common type of share. Every limited company must have ordinary shares. They are paid dividends if there are profits and cash available. Preferred shares usually pay a fixed rate of dividend. They are entitled to repayment of capital before ordinary shares if the company is wound up. They have preferential rights to dividends if there are sufficient profits and cash.

3 False. Debentures are not part of equity. Equity is made up of all permanent share capital plus reserves.

4 Capital.

5 Bank loans, legacies and so on.

6 Payments for the holiday and television set are drawings.

7 Wages £77470 (£77360 + £1450 − £1340).

8 False. Capital accounts record deliberate injections of capital and any changes to the value of assets (including goodwill). Current accounts detail entries relating to the current year's profit/losses, drawings and changes due to errors in previous years' income statements.

9 Capital accounts show capital transactions. Current accounts record the profits earned by each partner (less drawings). If a partner draws more from the business than is earned, this is easily recognised and it does not deplete the permanent capital of the business.

10 A's balance of £3000 should be shared between the remaining partners in the ratio represented by the capital account balances shown on the last statement of financial position. So, B will be debited with £1200 and C with £1800.

11 £2.50 each (£150000 ÷ £60000).

12 Published accounts are part of the stewardship function of accounting, showing the owners (shareholders) how the company is run. Competitors could gain access to this information, so details need to be protected by producing an abridged version.

13 Auditors are appointed by the shareholders. They scrutinise the financial statements to ensure that they give a true and fair view of the company's activities.

14 Schedule of non-current assets.

Vehicles	
Cost or valuation	£
At start of period	140000
Additions	20000
Disposals	(12000)
At end of period	148000

15 False. A statement of cash flows is an historic document. It details the cash inflows and cash outflows that have already taken place during the previous accounting period.

16 Purchase of the vehicle; dividends received.

17 O; I; O; No cash involved; I; I; I; I.

18 Depreciation is added to operating profit because it has reduced profit but not cash. Depreciation is the apportioning of the cost of an asset during its useful lifetime. It is not a cache of money available for replacement.

19 They provide the ground rules used in preparing financial statements. They should be applied uniformly throughout the business world, allowing comparisons to be made more easily.

20 Accruals; consistency; prudence.

21 Recoverable amount is the value in use £120000; impairment is £20000 (£140000 − £120000).

22 Answers could include, for example, trademarks, goodwill, patents, copyrights.

23 AVCO and FIFO.

24 A periodic method uses one valuation that takes place generally at a financial year end. A perpetual method records every individual transaction that involves inventory movements and values the goods after each purchase.
   Periodic – small independent take-away.
   Perpetual – national chain of supermarkets.

25 £54200 (£54000 + £800 − £600).

Page numbers in **bold** refer to **key terms definitions**.

Index